Property Management
and Managing Risk

ROBERT C. KYLE and

FLOYD M. BAIRD, RPA/SMA

MARIE S. SPODEK, DREI,
Consulting Editor

Dearborn™
Real Estate Education

President: Mehul Patel
Executive Director of Product Development: Kate DeVivo
Managing Editor: Anne Huston
Managing Editor: Tony Peregrin
Development Editor: Liz Austin
Director of Production: Daniel Frey
Senior Managing Editor, Print Production: Jack Kiburz
Production Artist: Cepheus Edmondson
Creative Director: Lucy Jenkins
Vice President of Product Management: Dave Dufresne
Director of Product Management: Melissa Kleeman

Published by Dearborn™ Real Estate Education
30 South Wacker Drive
Chicago, Illinois 60606-7481
(312) 836-4400
www.dearbornRE.com

11   10   9   8   7   6   5   4

ISBN-13: 978-1-4277-7097-4

ISBN-10: 1-4277-7097-2

preface   v
about the authors   vi
acknowledgments   vii

Chapter 1

Introduction to Professional Property Management   1

Key Terms   1
Introduction to Property Management   2
Classification of Real Property   2
Duties of the Property Manager   7
Case Study   10
Summary   11
Review Questions   12

Chapter 2

The Manager-Owner Relationship   14

Key Terms   14
Nature of the Relationship   14
Takeover Procedures   23
Case Study   25
Summary   26
Review Questions   27

Chapter 3

Economics and Planning   29

Key Terms   29
Economics and Planning   30
The Management Plan   33
Market Analysis   33
Property Analysis   35
Analysis of the Owner's Objectives   37
Preparing the Management Plan   37
Case Study   41
Summary   42
Review Questions   43

Chapter 4   **Leases and Tenant Issues 45**

Key Terms 45

Leasehold Estates 46

Types of Lease Payments 48

Essential Provisions of a Valid Lease 49

Managing Tenant Relations 56

Case Study 59

Summary 60

Review Questions 61

Chapter 5   **Managing Residential Properties 64**

Key Terms 64

Residential Housing: The Big Picture 64

Types of Residential Property 65

Tenant Relations and Fair Housing Laws 68

Residential Market Analysis 72

Maintaining the Apartment Building 73

Apartment Operating Reports 73

Operating Budgets and Reports in Condos and Co-Ops 77

Management Fees 78

Case Study 78

Summary 80

Review Questions 82

Chapter 6   **Managing Risk and Tenant Safety Issues 84**

Key Terms 84

Risk Management 85

Managing Environmental Issues 87

Managing Life Safety and Security 88

Role of Personnel in Life Safety 90

Property Management Procedures 91

Minimizing Post-Emergency Damage 93

Criminal Activity Issues 94

Case Study 95

Summary 95

Review Questions 97

glossary 99

answer key 103

Index 115

Property management is a highly specialized but rapidly growing sector of the real estate profession. As a real estate licensee, you may not be a property manager yourself, but you are likely to work closely with property managers at some point. It is important to learn the basic principles underlying property management and to recognize the issues that property managers deal with.

This book provides an overview of the property management field and describes the major functions of property managers. Its emphasis is on real-life practice, not on theories or generalities. It is intended for the real estate professional who wants a comprehensive introduction to the challenging field of property management.

The text addresses issues of concern to commercial real estate agents who manage large properties, as well as to licensees who own or manage a few small properties on a personal or informal basis. Obviously, some information will be more relevant to one type of manager than another, but many fundamental principles and practices are equally important to both.

■ Structure and Features

Each chapter begins with a list of key terms and concrete learning objectives, and every chapter concludes with a case study, a summary of the most important issues, and a series of questions to test your comprehension. The special feature "Liability Alert!" details risk management tips that can assist in controlling the risk of exposure to lawsuits from both owners and tenants, hopefully avoiding the spiraling costs of legal liability. Managing liability is a particularly key issue for licensees who spread their efforts between sales and property managers. Throughout this book, look for Liability Alerts! for relevant suggestions about controlling (or avoiding) exposure to liability.

Each chapter includes a case study drawn from the authors' experience in the property management field, complete with questions to spark discussion and debate or just to get you thinking about how to apply what you've learned in your own property management work.

Robert C. Kyle, MA, MBA, DBA, is the principal author of *Modern Real Estate Practice.* Mr. Kyle is past president of the Association of Illinois Real Estate Educators and the national Real Estate Educators Association, from which he received the Emeritus Award.

Floyd M. Baird, AB, JD, DREI, was vice president and manager of Trust Real Estate for Liberty Bancorp, Inc., of Oklahoma City and Tulsa, where he was responsible for over 750 properties, and national director of the Building Owners and Managers Institute.

The authors would like to thank the following reviewers who contributed helpful feedback and guidance during the development of this edition:

■ Karen R. Post, Post Exchange, REALTORS®

■ Patricia L. Trombello, CPM, Technical Training Consultants, Inc.

The authors and the publisher would also like to extend special thanks to Marie Spodek, DREI, GRI, for serving as consulting editor on this edition. A popular and nationally known real estate educator and sales trainer, Ms. Spodek is an active member of the Real Estate Educators Association and the National Association of REALTORS®. Her invaluable professional advice and sound judgment are greatly appreciated.

chapter one

Introduction to Professional Property Management

■ Key Terms

Americans with
  Disabilities Act (ADA)

antitrust laws

asset management
  services

commercial property

concierge services

disability

Equal Credit Opportunity
  Act (ECOA)

Fair Housing Act (Title VIII
  of the Civil Rights Act of
  1968)

familial status

incubator space

industrial property

Lead-Based Paint
  Hazard Reduction Act
  (LBPHRA)

leasing agent

manufactured home park

Megan's law

ministorage facilities

office property

real property

research and
  development centers

residential property

retail property

special-purpose property

learning objectives

On completing this chapter, you will be able to

■ state the three primary goals of a property manager;

■ list four classifications of real property and give examples of each;

■ explain the difference between office property and retail property;

■ recognize the importance of understanding the owner's objectives;

■ state the reason for antitrust laws and give an example of what not to discuss
with competitors;

■ explain why retail and office building managers must understand the Americans with Disabilities Act (ADA); and

■ differentiate between the protected classes of fair housing laws and those protected under the Equal Credit Opportunity Act (ECOA).

■ Introduction to Property Management

A *property manager* is a person who manages real estate on behalf of the owner for compensation. A property manager's primary function is threefold:

1. Achieve the owner's objectives
2. Generate income for the owners
3. Preserve and/or enhance the value of the property

In other words, *the manager attempts to generate the greatest possible net income for the owners of an investment property over that property's useful life.* Managers must be skilled in working with the owners (Chapter 2), financial plans and reports (Chapter 3), and tenants (Chapter 4). In reality, the property manager's job is far more demanding than simply showing available space, executing leases, and colleting rents.

Property management, one of the fastest-growing areas of specialization within the real estate industry, is emerging as a managerial science. Today, property managers must have the knowledge, communication skills, and technical expertise needed to be dynamic decision makers. They may be called on to act as market analysts, advertising executives, salespeople, accountants, diplomats, or even maintenance engineers. Interpersonal skills are needed to deal effectively with owners, prospects, tenants, employees, outside contractors, and others in the real estate business. Above all, the property manager in the 21st century must be versatile.

■ Classification of Real Property

Real property is defined as the earth's surface extending downward to the center of the earth and upward into space, including all things permanently attached to it naturally or artificially. Given this comprehensive definition, it follows that real property management can cover a wide spectrum of duties.

Types of Real Property

For property management purposes, real estate can be divided into four major classifications: residential, commercial, industrial, and special-purpose property. Each type of property requires a different combination of knowledge and skills on the part of the manager.

Residential property.   Residential real estate, including privately owned residences as well as government and institutional housing, satisfies the basic shelter needs of our population. (See Figure 1.1.) It is the largest source of demand for the services of professional property managers. Residential real property can take several different forms:

■ **Single-family homes.** According to the Census Bureau, more 60 percent of U.S. housing is owner occupied. Single-family, owner-occupied homes typically do not require professional management, but more owners of the

Figure 1.1 | The Three Categories of Residential Property

| Single-family homes | Duplexes and triplexes | Apartments |

Residential property can be broadly grouped into three categories.

10 percent of properties that are rentals are hiring professional managers, particularly rentals of manufactured home parks, condominiums, and vacation homes. Also, many owners of very small apartment buildings, such as duplexes, triplexes, and fourplexes, may also likely to hire professional management.

■ **Manufactured home parks.** Manufactured homes are built in factories to Department of Housing and Urban Development (HUD) specifications. While permanently attached to a chassis that, in theory, permits them to be moved, fewer than 5 percent of manufactured homes are moved a second time. About one-third are sited in rental communities, and their value comes from the desirability of the community. Most are owner managed, but professionals manage the others. The manufactured home owner either rents the land or rents the home and the land. Many retirees in the Sun Belt states live in manufactured home parks, especially those that have been designated "senior" living (near elderly is older than 55; elderly is older than 62).

■ **Multifamily residences.** Rising land and construction costs have stimulated the growth of multifamily housing. The economy of design and land usage inherent in multifamily housing allows for a lower per-family cost of construction. Thus, multifamily residences are a rapidly growing segment of the national residential real estate market. Multifamily residences have many classifications—among them are garden developments, walkup buildings, and highrise buildings. (See Figure 1.2.)

■ **Facilities for the aging.** The growing numbers of aging baby boomers is fueling the need for retirement communities, homes for the aged, convalescent care facilities, and independent living facilities.

Figure 1.2 | Residential Real Estate Categories

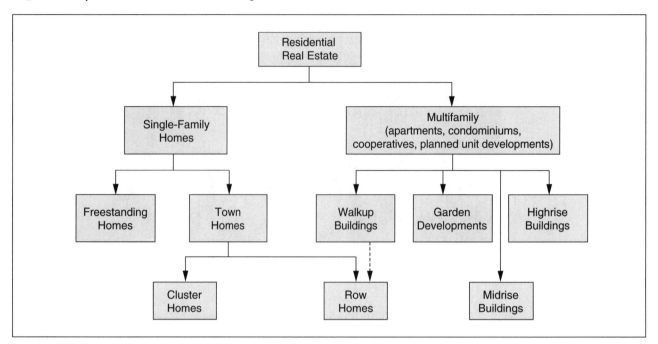

Liability Alert!

Comply with Applicable Laws

Most of all, managers should strive to remain current by attending continuing education classes and classes at trade shows. Managers should stress compliance at every opportunity with every employee and keep copies of any training sessions held.

Federal and state **antitrust laws** apply to property managers, real estate agents, steel and oil companies, and most interstate industry. Managers must be careful that they do not even appear to be setting rents and fees in collusion with other managers.

The federal **Americans with Disabilities Act (ADA)** is most applicable to commercial properties, including retail and office spaces. The ADA requires that public accommodations be readily accessible to anyone without regard to **disability**, that is, to anyone with any physical or mental impairment that substantially limits one or more of an individual's major life activities.

The **Fair Housing Act (Title VIII of the Civil Rights Act of 1968)** prohibits discrimination in housing on the basis of race, color, religion, national origin, sex, disability, and familial status; **familial status** refers to a household in which at least one person under the age of 18 is living. State laws and local ordinances often add additional protections, including sexual preference. Some states also include protections against similar discrimination in commercial rental properties.

Property managers must avoid even the appearance of discrimination in advertising and showing residential properties or in offering and enforcing residential leases. Civil penalties include fines ranging from $11,000 for the first offense to more than $55,000 for multiple offenses within a seven-year period, in addition to awarding actual and punitive (unlimited) damages to the aggrieved parties.

The **Equal Credit Opportunity Act (ECOA)** prohibits discrimination based on certain, defined, protected classes when applying for financing, whether for a loan to buy a house or for credit for a lease. These protected categories include race, color, religion, national origin, sex, receipt of public assistance, age, and marital status.

All managers in every state must comply with the regulations of the federal **Lead-Based Paint Hazard Reduction Act (LBPHRA).** The disclosures of possible lead-based paint must be made to any residential tenant, whether in a multifamily property or in a single residence that was built prior to 1978. Fines for failure to disclose possible contamination range from $11,000 to $66,000.

Under **Megan's law** requirements, certain sex offenders must register with local law enforcement agencies. Property managers may wish to include a criminal background check as part of the hiring process for employees who have keys and access to apartments, particularly if access is not always supervised. Owners and managers should do everything possible so that the key to a resident's home does not end up in the hands of a registered sex offender.

Commercial property. Commercial real estate includes various types of income-producing properties, such as office buildings, shopping centers, stores, gas stations, and parking lots. (See Figure 1.3.)

Figure 1.3 | Commercial Real Estate Categories

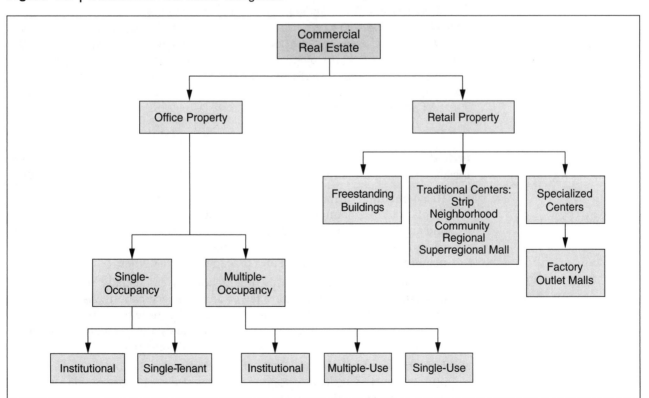

Commercial real estate is generally divided into three categories: office, retail, and research and development:

1. **Office property.** Office property can be lowrise (walkup) offices, garden developments, highrise complexes, or office parks (sometimes called *business parks*). Whether an office property is situated in a downtown commercial district or in a suburban development, its success is determined by its location relative to the prospective workforce, transportation facilities, and other business services. Office property can have several tenants or a single occupant.

2. **Retail property.** Retail property, where goods are sold, includes freestanding buildings, traditional shopping centers, malls, and specialized centers.

3. **Research and development centers.** Research centers, which are also called **incubator spaces,** are often located in the same locale as universities with active graduate schools. Tenants may specialize in certain fields, such as high-tech computing or engineering. The traditional separation between office space and manufacturing or warehouse facilities is breaking down in many business and industrial parks that now offer combinations of office and industrial space or buildings divided into differently sized units for incubator spaces to adapt to the changing needs of a growing company.

Liability Alert!

Comply with the ADA

A commercial property is generally considered to be a "public accommodation"—a private entity that provides goods, services, facilities, or accommodations to the public. Thus, even though commercial services are privately owned, the public has certain rights to use them. Title III of the Americans with Disabilities Act (ADA) requires accessibility to everyone. The ADA requires managers to ensure that people with disabilities have full and equal access to facilities and services offered by any public accommodation. ADA experts should be consulted, as well as architectural designers who specialize in accessibility issues. The property manager typically is responsible for determining whether a building meets the ADA's requirements and for retrofitting or remodeling a building that is not in compliance. Often this requires negotiations as to who is responsible for paying for the changes: the owner or the tenant.

Industrial property.   Industrial property includes all land and facilities used for heavy and light manufacturing, for storage, and for the distribution of goods:

■ **Heavy manufacturing.** Industrial plants, such as steel mills, automotive plants, and petroleum refineries, require access to transportation facilities and an adequate source of raw materials. Because property for heavy industry must be designed with the specific needs of potential users in mind, such plants are generally occupied and managed by the owner.

■ **Light manufacturing.** Assembly or warehousing can usually be performed in smaller buildings that require fewer unique specifications. As a result, light industrial buildings can often be utilized by more than one type of enterprise—a fact that has stimulated some real estate speculators to build this type of facility for future lease to industrial concerns.

■ **Industrial parks.** Industrial parks that include extensive office space are often referred to as business parks. They are often one-story plants and include ample parking and extensive landscaping.

- **Ministorage facilities.** Often, these are storage areas not specifically designed to meet the needs of industry (i.e., warehouses) but for extra storage space for homeowners, apartment dwellers, and businesses that store files, extra supplies, and surplus equipment. Many of these locations require that the managers live on-site.

- **Others.** Loft buildings in the older parts of urban areas are converted into various combinations of manufacturing, office, residential, and storage space. Distribution facilities to relieve traffic congestion of the central city are located at transportation hubs in suburban industrial parks. Management responsibilities are often shared by landlord and tenant.

Special-purpose property. Hotels, motels, clubs, resorts, nursing homes, manufactured home parks, theaters, schools, colleges, government institutions, and places of worship are considered special-purpose property. The common denominator is the fact that the activity taking place in these buildings is a special business or organizational undertaking that dictates the design and operation of the buildings themselves.

■ Duties of the Property Manager

Just as there are various types of real property, there are also different classifications of property managers. A professional property manager may be an individual entrepreneur, a member of a real estate firm specializing in property management, or a member of the property management department of a large multiservice real estate company. The manager also may work within the trust department of a financial institution or within the real estate department of a large corporation or public institution. The manager should identify and analyze the owner's goals, which will vary widely among the individual, corporate, fiduciary, and government owners.

Here are just some of the niche markets:

- **Concierge services.** Today, concierges offer available services to the tenants in office buildings. Services can offer fax, courier, and secretarial aid; cater in-office lunches and arrange conferences; and provide rental service for little-used office equipment. Sometimes, they even offer personal services, such as shopping, automobile care, dry cleaning, and more.

- **Asset management services.** Typically, asset management in the real estate context refers to financial management of a sizable number of investment properties. These managers often supervise deals and are responsible for a portfolio of properties, rather than managing a single property, and will likely monitor financial performance, study local markets, and compare individual properties against a norm. Like the financial asset manager, the real property asset manager usually has a strong voice in retaining or disposing of property.

- **Corporate property managers.** The corporate property manager helps create facilities and then manages properties for corporations that invest in real estate. Inasmuch as real estate is not the primary activity for the corporation, professional property managers are required. Companies may downsize and reduce staff or hire outsiders to manage. Either way, professional managers are necessary.

■ **Technology experts.** Property managers must be on the cutting edge of technology, particularly those involved with smart buildings, since everything in a building is technology based: elevators, heating and air conditioning, security, and more.

■ **Leasing agents.** Those skilled in taking a prospect to a signed lease are in great demand, especially in a very competitive market. Many of these agents move from property to property and are usually paid by commission.

Liability Alert!

Comply with State Licensing Laws

Real estate license laws about who needs to be licensed before managing properties vary greatly among states. Generally, a person needs a real estate license to list or offer to list a property for sale, rent, or exchange, or even to offer to engage in such activities. However, there may be vast differences from state to state as to who really needs a license, and if so, what kind.

A few states do not regulate property management activities in any way; others require a broker's license to collect rent, negotiate leases, show properties for rent, and more. Some states require that a manager of a condominium community or cooperative building must have at least a broker's license (or work directly under one) or a certification that requires more education and experience. South Carolina has created a separate license for those who only manage properties, with no listing and selling involvement. Often, those who work "directly" for an owner are exempt from licensing requirements, as are resident managers, attorneys, and those managing properties owned by the government.

Another very important issue is handling rents and security deposits, especially residential security deposits. Most state laws require that such funds must be deposited in trust accounts, strictly monitored for safe keeping.

Regardless of their employment background, property managers pursue similar objectives. Although specific management duties will vary according to the situation and particular property, the successful manager must be competent in all of these areas. These areas include:

■ Planning

■ Advertising and merchandising

■ Screening tenants

■ Negotiating leases

■ Collecting rent

■ Maintaining the premises

■ Supervising security

■ Obtaining insurance

■ Paying taxes on the property

■ Keeping accurate records

■ Making periodic reports to the property owner

In addition to the tasks directly involved in property management, professional managers should take an interest in professional, social, and political organizations in their municipalities. Their long-range goals will be more easily realized if property managers take on civic responsibilities and help to implement plans for the growth and improvement of their communities.

Liability Alert!

Evaluate the Owner's Objectives

Some owners will direct a property manager to operate a property so as to extract every possible dollar from it. This direction may not actually be expressed, but it is evidenced by an owner who demands frequent payments of accumulated cash, refuses to make any but the most necessary repairs, and pays bills at the last possible minute. This is called *milking a property*. A property manager in this position should point out the ultimate loss that can occur as a result of following such a course of action. If the owner continues to direct that the property be managed in this manner, the manager should document the owner's direction in writing and consider whether to continue managing the property under policies that doom it to financial failure.

Professional Organizations and Designations

Many growth opportunities exist for those who wish to specialize in managing properties, ranging from various types of residential properties to shopping centers to office buildings and more. Although the organizations geared toward commercial management are older, more organizations are geared to residential rentals, in large part because the majority of rental properties are residential.

Building Owners and Managers Association International (BOMA) (*www.boma.org*).   In the early 20th century, George A. Holt, owner and manager of a Chicago skyscraper, invited his colleagues to a dinner at which the Chicago Building Managers Organization was born. The organization held its first national meeting in 1908. By 1921, a number of groups had formed in the nation's larger cities and organizational changes were required: the Building Owners and Managers Association (BOMA) became a national federation of local and regional groups. Later, as chapters were organized in Canada, England, South Africa, Japan, and Australia, the name was changed to the Building Owners and Managers Association (BOMA) International.

Building Owners and Managers Institute (*www.bomi.org*).   An independent organization, the Building Owners and Managers Institute (BOMI) was established in 1970 to offer educational programs for property owners and managers of commercial properties. Today, it offers professional designations based on experience and successful completion of its courses in all areas of managing commercial properties. Consult *www.bomi.org* for a complete list. Its most prestigious designation is Real Property Administrator (RPA).

Institute of Real Estate Management (IREM) (*www.irem.org*).   In 1933, a group of property management firms created the Institute of Real Estate Management (IREM), which is today an affiliate group of the National Association of Realtors® (NAR). IREM offers opportunities for managers to meet to share ideas and offers education programs. IREM offers the designation of Certified Property Manager (CPM) to those who meet educational, experience, and examination requirements. It grants qualified management firms the designation of Accredited Management Organization (AMO®).

International Council of Shopping Centers (ICSC) (*www.icsc.org*). The International Council of Shopping Centers (ICSC), formed in 1957, links together more than 25 national and regional shopping center councils in more than 80 countries. Its certification programs are based on the application of knowledge and skill. Its most recognized and valuable certification is the Certified Shopping Center Manager (CSM), which is supplemented by other specialty courses and certifications.

National Apartment Association (NAA) (*www.naahq.org*). The National Apartment Association (NAA) grew out of problems that residential rental property owners and managers faced during the Depression. It sponsors courses for managers, such as those with the Certified Apartment Manager designation and others.

National Multi Housing Council (*www.nmhc.org*). The National Multi Housing Council offers extensive training for those involved in managing larger apartment complexes. Its certification programs offer industry professionals a training path for complete career development. The Registered Apartment Manager (RAM) certification is the oldest residential property management certification program in the United States. The certification is also approved by the Department of Housing and Urban Development (HUD) as providing quality training to managers of multifamily rental, condominium, cooperative, subsidized, and market-rate housing. The council also offers many more designations for specialized proponents of managing large apartment communities.

National Association of Residential Property Managers (NARPM) (*www.narpm.org*). The National Association of Residential Property Managers (NARPM) was founded in 1988 as a trade association to assist managers of single-family homes and small apartment buildings. Today, it offers the Residential Management Professional (RMP) designation, which is based on current managing experience and successful completion of its educational program, and other designations for specialty niches.

case study

As soon as she graduated from college, Janet Lance worked for a major commercial property management company. Her duties as a third-party manager included scheduling and supervising the management operations of three of the properties in the company's portfolio: an apartment building, a small strip mall, and an office building. She monitored the properties through on-site agents' reports.

After a couple of years, Janet found that she not only liked office building management, but also had demonstrated a real talent for handling the many varied duties and responsibilities of a property manager. Through contacts developed in professional organizations, Janet was hired to manage on-site a large single-occupant landmark office building.

After some years there, however, she discovered that she missed the variety of duties of third-party management. She accepted a position as the chief asset manager for a large commercial investor that owned extensive rental properties throughout the western United States. Janet now oversees the operations of several dozen property managers and a staff of several hundred.

Case Study Review

1. Which law is *MOST* vital to comply with when managing an office building?

    a. Fair housing law

    b. Equal Credit Opportunity Act (ECOA)

    c. Americans with Disabilities Act (ADA)

    d. Lead-Based Hazard Reduction Act

2. Unlike a residential property manager, an asset manager must be skilled in

    a. screening tenants.

    b. collecting rents.

    c. advertising a vacancy.

    d. reading and acting on financial reports.

■ Summary

Individuals who have completed BOMA International's educational program through its institute are awarded the designation of Real Property Administrator (RPA). In 1933, the Institute of Real Estate Management (IREM) was formed as a subsidiary body of the National Association of REALTORS® (NAR). The designation of Certified Property Manager (CPM) was adopted in 1938 to denote individuals who had successfully fulfilled all of the necessary requirements to gain admission to IREM.

For the purposes of professional property management, real estate can be divided into four major classifications: residential, commercial, industrial, and special-purpose property. Each requires a different combination of knowledge and skills from the manager.

Residential real estate is the single largest area of involvement for property managers. The rapid rise in land and construction costs has created a demand for rentals of single-family and small apartment buildings and also multifamily residences and a corresponding demand for qualified managers. Other areas of specialization include managing manufactured home parks and many aspects of renting to baby boomers.

Commercial real estate consists of office buildings and retail property. Most office space is leased to one or more tenant businesses. Retail property includes free-standing stores and restaurants, commercial strip centers, neighborhood centers, community centers, and large shopping malls. Industrial property includes heavy and light manufacturing plants, along with warehouses for storage and distribution of products.

State laws vary greatly as to license requirements for managing properties, so anyone who is planning to enter the field should start with contacting the state regulatory agency. State laws also regulate the receipt of rent and security deposits and the return of the latter.

■ Review Questions

True-False

1. A property manager's three main responsibilities are to generate income on behalf of the owners, achieve the owner's objectives, and preserve the property's value.
   a. True
   b. False

2. AMO is one of the professional organizations available to professional property managers.
   a. True
   b. False

3. Commercial real estate includes hotels, nursing homes, and theaters.
   a. True
   b. False

4. According to the U.S. Census Bureau, 80 percent of U.S. housing is owner occupied.
   a. True
   b. False

5. The Americans with Disabilities Act (ADA) prohibits discrimination in residential properties.
   a. True
   b. False

6. Retirement homes are examples of special-use properties.
   a. True
   b. False

7. Federal fair housing laws prohibit a manager from refusing to rent to a person based on his or her religion or color.
   a. True
   b. False

8. The owner who takes money from the property and does not make any needed repairs is said to be milking the property.
   a. True
   b. False

9. A commercial property is generally subject to accessibility requirements of the Americans with Disabilities Act (ADA).
   a. True
   b. False

10. Not every property manager must be licensed by the state.
    a. True
    b. False

Multiple-Choice

1. The primary function of the property manager is to
   a. rent units for owners.
   b. generate the greatest income for owner.
   c. show space to prospective tenants.
   d. decrease the value of the property.

2. In today's market, what skills are required of a successful property manager?
   a. Highly versatile and skilled in multiple areas of expertise
   b. Highly specialized and capable of working only as a market analyst or financial planner
   c. Prepared to work behind the scenes, allowing the tenants and owners to freely interact
   d. Able to show available space and talk prospective tenants into renting a space

3. Rising land and construction costs have stimulated the growth of
   a. facilities for the aging.
   b. manufactured home parks.
   c. highrise luxury condominium properties.
   d. multifamily residences.

4. The largest demand for the services of the professional property manager is found in what type of property?
   a. Residential
   b. Commercial
   c. Industrial
   d. Government

5. Federal fair housing laws prohibit discrimination in housing based on
   a. sexual preference.
   b. age.
   c. marital status.
   d. familial status.

6. Civil penalties for violations of the federal fair housing law include
   a. imprisonment up to three years.
   b. unlimited fines.
   c. $11,000 to $55,000 in fines.
   d. up to $100,000 for the first fine.

7. Commercial real estate includes
   a. apartment buildings.
   b. farms.
   c. mines.
   d. office buildings.

8. The Americans with Disabilities Act (ADA) is *MOST* applicable to managers of
   a. multifamily residential properties.
   b. farms.
   c. commercial properties.
   d. industrial properties.

9. Shopping centers, factory outlets, and superregional malls are examples of
   a. special-purpose properties.
   b. distribution facilities.
   c. office property.
   d. retail property.

10. Many business parks offer a combination of office and industrial space that is divided into units of various sizes. These spaces are called
    a. loft buildings.
    b. research and development centers.
    c. ministorage.
    d. light industrial.

11. Properties designed to meet specific needs of heavy industry are generally
    a. developed by real estate speculators.
    b. managed by large real estate companies.
    c. occupied and managed by the owner.
    d. sold to investors and leased back.

12. All of the following are examples of concierge services *EXCEPT* offering
    a. business services to tenants—fax or courier service.
    b. rental services of small equipment to tenants.
    c. personal services such as picking up cleaning, gift wrapping, and shopping.
    d. extra storage space.

13. The professional manager, acting as agent for the owner, should
    a. lay out a business plan according to business school standards.
    b. recognize what the owner wants to achieve.
    c. help the owner recognize the superiority of the manager's experiences.
    d. not bother the owner with too many reports and plans.

14. Which organization is an affiliate of the National Association of REALTORS®?
    a. BOMA International
    b. Institute of Real Estate Management (IREM)
    c. National Apartment Association (NAA)
    d. National Multi Housing Council

15. The oldest residential property management certification program in the United States that is HUD-approved is
    a. Certified Apartment Manager (CAM).
    b. Professional Property Manager (PPM).
    c. Registered Apartment Manager (RAM).
    d. Accredited Residential Manager (ARM).

chapter two

The Manager-Owner Relationship

■ Key Terms

agent   fiduciary duties   principal

commingling   general agent   special agent

employee   management contract

employer   percentage fees

learning objectives

On completing this chapter, you will be able to

■ contrast the differences between employer-employee and principal-agent relationships;

■ discuss the fiduciary responsibilities of the agent to the principal, which are care, obedience, accounting, loyalty, and disclosure;

■ recognize that property managers must comply with state statutes with regard to licensing requirements;

■ name the essential elements of a typical property management contract;

■ list the information required from the owner when taking over a new property; and

■ summarize the value of monthly reports and personal contact with the owner.

■ Nature of the Relationship

After the property manager and the owner agree on principles, objectives, and a viable management plan, they must then agree on the structure of their relationship, their specific responsibilities and liabilities, the scope of the manager's authority, fees, and the duration of their relationship.

The manager and the owner must work out the structure of their relationship. Three basic relationships can exist between a property manager and the individual or corporate owner of a building:

1. Employer-employee relationship
2. Formal fiduciary relationship (trust)
3. Principal-agent relationship

Employer-Employee Relationship

The employer-employee relationship is usually found in banks, colleges, large corporations, and other private institutions that require managerial services for their properties. The **employee**-manager is directly responsible to the officers of the owner-**employer** corporation or institution, which may be the principal occupant of the property.

Liability Alert!

Employee-Employer Relationships

Although no formalized contract is necessary in an employer-employee relationship, certain issues should be clarified in writing. At the least, the manager should obtain from the employing corporation written authorization to sign binding leases. Employee-managers are often limited in the dollar amount or length of lease that they are authorized to sign. Many lessees, especially government agencies and corporations, request a copy of this authorization from the employee-manager.

Formal Fiduciary, or Trust, Relationship

A trust is a device by which one person or institution transfers legal ownership of property to someone else to hold or manage for the benefit of a third party. For example, many banks, trust companies, and employee benefit and pension plans have acquired income property that they hold in trust, and many investors use established forms of trust to help meet their investment goals.

It is not possible to examine this form of ownership fully in this text because the trustee is governed by the terms of the trust instrument itself and federal and state laws concerning trusts. If employee benefit plans are involved, the trustee is also regulated by the U.S. Department of Labor.

Liability Alert!

Special Duties of Trustees

A trustee is governed not only by the terms of the trust instrument itself but also by federal and state laws concerning trusts, by banking and securities regulations, and in the case of employee benefit plans, by the U.S. Department of Labor. Property managers must take special precautions to learn and define the legal responsibilities and requirements of the relationship.

Principal-Agent Relationship

The principal-agent relationship is usually created by a written contract signed by both parties and empowers the property manager, as agent, to act on behalf of the owner, or **principal,** in certain situations. Specifically, the agent acts on behalf of the principal to bring him or her into legal relations with third parties. The written agreement creating this relationship is called the management contract; it empowers the property manager, as agent, to act on behalf of the owner, or principal, in certain situations. The agent is governed by the terms of the contract and by certain legal and ethical considerations based on the law of agency.

Liability Alert!

Be Aware of an Agent's Duties

Implicit in the principal-agent relationship are certain legal and ethical considerations that the property manager owes to the owner. These considerations (called **fiduciary duties**) are based on the law of agency.

In addition, each state has various licensing laws and regulations governing the conduct of persons and organizations acting as real estate agents. Although these laws apply mainly to sales of real estate, property managers are often covered as well. A few states have adopted statutes and administrative rules that apply solely to property managers. Property managers should investigate the statutes of the states where they manage property to be sure they are in compliance with those laws.

Agency Responsibilities

Managers owe certain responsibilities to their principals, the parties who hire them. Generally, the scope of authority is defined in the **management contract** and often includes the common law fiduciary duties. Some states have abolished the common law duties, instead requiring that the duties be enumerated in the agreement.

Scope of agency authority. An **agent** is either a *general agent* or a *special agent* depending on the scope of the agent's authority. A **general agent** can act on behalf of the principal on a range of matters and can obligate the principal to any contracts signed by the agent that are within the scope of that agent's duties. On the other hand, a **special agent** is only authorized to represent the principal on a specific matter or transaction. Once that transaction is concluded, the agency is terminated. A special agent has no authority to sign any contracts on behalf of the principal. A property manager is usually a general agent because of the variety of tasks to be performed. (See Figure 2.1.)

Fiduciary duties. An agent, whether specific or general, has certain duties that are imposed by agency law. This is because an agent has a fiduciary relationship with his or her principal, a confidential relationship marked by trust and confidence that requires the highest degree of loyalty on the part of the agent. Implicit in this fiduciary relationship are other duties, including the following:

- **Loyalty.** The property manager must always put the property owner's interests first, above his or her own interests.
- **Care.** The property manager must exercise a reasonable degree of skill while managing the property.

Figure 2.1 | Types of Agency

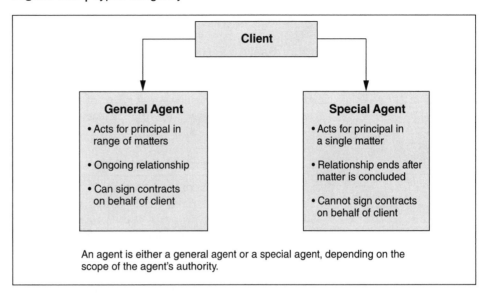

Client

General Agent
- Acts for principal in range of matters
- Ongoing relationship
- Can sign contracts on behalf of client

Special Agent
- Acts for principal in a single matter
- Relationship ends after matter is concluded
- Cannot sign contracts on behalf of client

An agent is either a general agent or a special agent, depending on the scope of the agent's authority.

Liability Alert!

Exercise the Duty of Care

If the property manager is careless in carrying out his or her duties, the property manager could be found negligent and be liable to the property owner for any damage.

■ **Obedience.** The property manager must carry out the property owner's lawful instructions.

Liability Alert!

"I Was Just Following Orders" Is No Defense

If the owner demands that the property manager do something that is illegal or unethical, the property manager should immediately terminate the relationship.

■ **Accounting.** The property manager must accurately report on the status of all funds received on behalf of or from the owner.

Liability Alert!

Don't Commingle Funds

State real estate licensing laws typically include detailed accounting requirements that must be followed explicitly by the property manager in regard to handling the principal's property or trust funds. These laws virtually always prohibit commingling by the property manager. **Commingling** involves combining the owner's funds with the property manager's business or personal funds.

■ **Disclosure.** The property manager must keep the owner fully informed of all material facts regarding the management of the property.

The management contract is a dated agreement signed by both the manager and the owner (or the owner's authorized representative) that defines the relationship between the parties, serves as a guide for the operation of the property, and provides a basis for the settlement of any future disputes. The terms of management contracts are as varied as the types of real property and the forms of real estate ownership. However, most management contracts share some basic, essential elements. (See Figure 2.2.)

Identification of the Parties and the Property

Most management contracts begin with an identification of the parties to the agreement. The owner's name ought to appear on the contract exactly as it does on the title or deed to the property. If the property is owned by a partnership, each partner's name should be stated in the contract and each should sign the document. When the property is owned by a corporation, the corporate name should appear on the contract, a duly authorized corporate officer should execute the agreement, and, where required, the corporate seal should be affixed to the document.

The street address of the property is often sufficient identification. Although a full legal description is not usually required, the property must be described so as to leave no doubt concerning its identity, location, and extent.

Contract Period

In addition to identifying the owner, manager, and specific property involved, the contract must stipulate a term of service. There is no single standard term for a management contract: its length depends on the size of the property, the responsibilities delegated to the manager, and the future intentions of the owner or owning body.

Liability Alert!

Termination Due to Owner Breach

Most agreements may be terminated before their expiration date by the agent if he or she suffers damages or liability as a result of the owner's failure to comply with any applicable statute, law, or government regulation. *Termination by the agent due to an owner's illegal acts does not release the owner from his or her obligations under the contract terms.*

Property Manager's Responsibilities

The manager is responsible for conveying to the owner information regarding the property. The following are just some of the reports that provide the owner with an idea of the status of the property and insight into the effectiveness of the manager.

Monthly reports and disbursements. A property manager must prepare a monthly earnings statement itemizing income and expenses for the property. The management contract should specify the name and address of the person, corporation, or board of directors (in the case of a cooperative or condominium) who is to receive the report, as well as the date on which it is to be submitted.

Figure 2.2 | Management Agreement

AGREEMENT TO MANAGE AND LEASE REAL ESTATE
(This is a legally binding contract. If you do not understand it, seek legal advice.)

This agreement to manage and lease real estate is made and entered into as of this _____ day of _____, _____ by and between _____ hereinafter called the Owner and _____ hereinafter called the Broker.

Whereas, Owner is the owner of the property known as _____ located at _____ and legally described as _____ _____ _____

Owner hereby employs Broker exclusively to rent, lease, operate and manage said property subject to the terms and conditions of this agreement.

In consideration of the management and leasing functions to be performed by Broker under this agreement, Owner agrees to pay Broker a fee or fees for services rendered at the rates hereinafter set forth. Owner recognizes Broker as agent in any negotiations relative to said property or any part thereof, which may have been initiated during the term hereof, and if consummated, shall compensate Broker in accordance with the rates hereinafter set forth. Such compensation is due and payable on demand and may be deducted by Broker from gross receipts.

Management: _____(plus sales tax)
Leasing: _____(plus sales tax)

The term of this agreement shall commence on the _____ day of _____, _____ and expire on the _____ day of _____, _____. This agreement is automatically renewable, upon expiration, for annual periods unless terminated by either party giving 30-days' written notice to the other party in advance of such termination date. However, the termination of this agreement shall not affect the right of Broker to receive leasing commissions or fees which have accrued on the date specified in such notice and have not been paid.

As agent for Owner, Broker owes Owner the duties of loyalty, obedience, disclosure, confidentiality, reasonable care and diligence, and full accounting. Broker must disclose all known material facts about the property which could affect a tenant's use or enjoyment of the property, disclose information which could have a material impact on either party's ability to fulfill their obligations under the lease agreement, respond honestly and accurately to questions concerning said property, and deal honestly and fairly with all parties.

The duties and responsibilities of Broker in connection with the management of said property are as follows:

1. Broker shall take all reasonable steps to collect and enforce the collection of all rentals and other charges due Owner from tenants of said property in accordance with the terms of their tenancies.

2. From gross revenues collected from said property, Broker is hereby authorized to accrue and make disbursements from Owner's funds for contractual mortgage payments, property and employee taxes, salaries and any other compensation due and payable to the employees of Owner, special assessments, premiums for hazard and liability insurance and any other insurance required, and sums otherwise due and payable by Owner as operating expenses which are incurred pursuant to the terms of this agreement including management and other fees as provided herein.

3. Broker shall deposit gross revenues collected into a special trust account in a bank whose deposits are insured by the Federal Deposit Insurance Corporation. Broker shall have authority to endorse checks payable to Owner, deposit funds of Owner into said trust account, and to draw on such account any payment to be made by Broker to discharge any of the liabilities or obligations incurred by Broker pursuant to this agreement.

4. Broker shall arrange all repairs, replacements and decorating necessary to maintain said property it its present condition and for the operating efficiency of said property. The expense of any one item of maintenance shall not exceed the sum of $_____ unless authorized by Owner or unless Broker determines it to be an emergency. Owner approval is not required in the event of an emergency where immediate repairs are required to preserve the property, continue essential services to the property, avoid danger to life or property, or to comply with federal, state or local law.

5. Broker shall have the authority to negotiate, prepare and execute all leases and to cancel and modify existing leases as agent for Owner.

Figure 2.2 | Management Agreement (Continued)

6. Broker shall advertise the availability for rent of the property or any part thereof and to display "For Rent" or "For Lease" signs thereon; to show property to prospective tenants; to execute leases, renewals or cancellations of leases relating to said property; to terminate tenancies and to sign and serve for Owner such notices as Broker deems appropriate; to institute legal actions in the name of Owner; to evict tenants and recover possession of said premises; to recover rents and other sums due, and to settle, compromise and release such actions.

7. Broker shall have authority to hire, supervise and terminate on behalf of Owner all independent contractors and property employees, if any, reasonably required in the operation of said property. All such property employees are employees of Owner.

8. Broker shall maintain accurate records of all moneys received and disbursed in connection with its management of said property, and such records shall be open for inspection by Owner at all reasonable times. Broker shall provide monthly financial statements to Owner.

Owner agrees to maintain a minimum balance of $_____ in Broker's trust account and in the event the amount falls below such minimum balance, Owner hereby agrees to pay such excess promptly upon the request of Broker.

Owner agrees to make available to Broker all data, records and documents pertaining to the property which Broker may require to properly exercise Broker's duties hereunder.

Owner shall complete and submit a lead-based paint disclosure if property is residential and built prior to 1978 as required by federal regulation.

Owner authorizes Broker to:
   a.   cooperate with brokers who represent tenants and
   b.   compensate cooperating brokers from Broker's fees
   c.   compensate Broker's agent

Owner agrees to hold Broker harmless from all damage suits in connection with the management of said property and from liability from injury suffered by any employee or other person whomsoever and to carry, at Owner's expense, adequate public liability insurance and to name Broker as co-insured. Broker also shall not be liable for any error of judgement oR for any mistake of fact or law, or for anything which Broker may do or refrain from doing hereunder, except in cases of willful misconduct or gross negligence. If suit is brought to collect Broker's compensation or if Broker successfully defends any action brought against Broker by Owner, relating to said property, or Broker's management thereof, Owner agrees to pay all costs incurred by Broker in connection with such action, including reasonable attorney fees.

This agreement may be later amended or modified at any time by a written mutual agreement signed by Owner and Broker.

Broker will not discriminate based on race, color, creed, religion, sex, national origin, age, handicap or familial status and will comply with all federal, state and local fair housing and civil rights laws and with all equal opportunity requirements.

Broker accepts this exclusive employment and agrees to use due diligence in the exercise of the duties, authority and powers conferred upon Broker under the terms hereof.

Receipt of a copy of the contract by the owner has been acknowledged.

_____   _____   _____   _____
Owner   Date   Owner   Date

_____   _____
Social Security Number or Tax Identification Number   Social Security Number or Tax Identification Number

_____   _____
Address   Phone Number

_____
City/State/Zipcode

_____ by _____
Broker   Agent

SDREC/PMAGENCY/OWNER/5-99   Page 2 of 2

Payments and other disbursements of funds. The names, addresses, and percentage amounts for all recipients to whom the agent must dispense monthly payments are usually listed in the contract. The contract should clarify the agent's obligations in months when disbursements exceed receipts. Under some contracts, the manager is authorized to hold a certain sum of money in reserve to meet expenses that may come due between the time of disbursements and the time the next monthly rental income flow begins. Most contracts (and most state laws) require the manager to maintain a separate bank account for the owner's funds; that is, the owner's funds should never be commingled with the agent's personal or business funds. If the manager works for more than one owner, it is wise to use an individual account for each.

Authority to rent, operate, and manage premises. The terms of the contract should list the agent's authority to lease, collect rents, terminate tenancies, return security deposits, evict tenants, and bring legal action for recovery of lost rents. The most important is the agent's authority to sign leases, for the statute of frauds in most states does not consider an oral lease agreement that is more than a certain duration (usually a year) to be enforceable.

Some contracts also contain a clause that gives the agent the power to enter into contracts not to exceed a certain amount for utility services, rubbish removal, window cleaning, or other recommended services. An owner might also set a ceiling on the advertising and marketing budget.

The terms of the management contract should also specify the agent's powers to hire and fire maintenance personnel for the premises. A manager who is permitted to hire the operating staff is usually expected not only to obtain liability and workers' compensation insurance for building personnel, but also to file returns and other reports required of the owner-employer by federal and state governments.

Owner's Responsibilities

The management agreement should spell out the owner's responsibility for miscellaneous management expenses. It should contain a clear statement designating the person responsible for each item of management and maintenance expenses, including the following:

- Payroll
- Insurance
- Purchasing
- Building
- Advertising
- Outside leasing agents

Scheduled payments. The owner should agree in the contract to give the agent a schedule of payments that must be made for debt service, taxes, special assessments, or insurance premiums. The manager can then budget or establish reserves for these items.

Repairs and maintenance. It is important for the management agreement to contain a clause that requires the owner to make any repairs and replacements necessary to keep the premises in their current condition and operating efficiently. The owner will be responsible for complying with the terms of the lease agreements, minimum housing codes, and any other applicable laws.

Management Fees of Independent Agent Managers

Management fees differ depending on the property. Apartment buildings pose different management problems from those of office buildings, just as inner-city property needs differ from suburban property needs. All contracts should specify the amount of the fee to be paid, when it is to be paid, and the manner of payment.

Flat or fixed fee versus percentage fee. Circumstances will dictate whether the management fee is to be paid by the flat-fee or the percentage method of compensation. A flat or fixed fee may be most appropriate when managing a condominium or cooperative community inasmuch as the owners want management to contain expenses, not increase them. The **percentage fee** is a wonderful incentive for the manager who needs to improve the income of the building, although a minimum fee may be established to protect management fees if the building revenue drops.

Liability Alert!

Compensation Method Does Not Limit Liability

A manager's legal and professional responsibility and liability as a fiduciary are the same regardless of the amount of compensation. In fact, a gratuitous agent (one who works for no fee at all) may be held liable for negligence in failing to perform a duty. The manager should clearly define the services to be rendered in managing a property, especially when dealing with a property with a marginal financial return.

Leasing fees.   Some owners are willing to pay a lump-sum fee or bonus when a new lease is executed or if the agent reaches certain lease-up goals. Especially with commercial properties, the leasing agent is not the only agent involved. Sometimes, the leasing fee is either split between the property manager and the leasing broker or wholly retained by the leasing broker. Or, the owner may agree to pay an additional amount when an outside broker or agent is involved. All possibilities should be thoroughly discussed and agreed on in the original management agreement.

Early termination.   In all circumstances, the manager should see that the contract contains a clause that provides adequate compensation for the leases that the manager has already negotiated, if the owner wants to terminate the contract prior to its scheduled cancellation date. The owner should be able to terminate the management agreement on service of proper notice as agreed to, and the agent should receive payment for negotiation of leases on behalf of the owner up to the date of termination.

Liability Alert!

Avoid Antitrust Violations

The fee structure must be negotiated between the owner and the manager and must be set independently. Fees must not be discussed with other, competing property management firms. If members of the property management profession try to impose uniform rates (or even appear to be establishing uniform rates), they will violate state and federal antitrust laws. Property managers may not suggest that a particular fee is "standard" and must avoid any discussions with competing firms that may even hint at collusion.

■ Takeover Procedures

Once the contract between the owner and the property manager has been signed, the transfer of responsibility for the property from the owner (or the current manager) should take place as soon as possible. The owner is responsible for providing the manager or management agency with all data necessary for the efficient operation of the property. The necessary information includes the following:

- Property address
- Title holder
- Owner's name
- Owner's address
- Owner's phone/fax/e-mail

- Where to send statements/vouchers
- Property identification number
- Owner's insurance broker
- Mortgagee
- Amount and due date of loan payments
- Utility account numbers
- Scavenger service
- Exterminator service
- Other service contractors
- Copies of employment tax records
- Current real estate tax bills
- Power of attorney for taxes
- Accounts payable ledger
- Building number
- Owner's attorney/accountant
- Apartment size
- Rental rates
- Names of present tenants
- Copies of all leases/special clauses
- Security deposits
- Current vacancies

After receiving the necessary information from the owner, the manager must set up accounting records and give notice of the takeover to all suppliers, service contractors, on-site employees, and tenants. The manager should personally inspect the property as part of the takeover.

Liability Alert!

Account for Tenant Security Deposits

Tenant security deposit balances and accounting are an essential part of any takeover. In many states, failure to return deposits or pay interest when required is a violation of the landlord-tenant law and is grounds for disciplinary action against the real estate licensee in addition to costly monetary damages.

Continuing Owner-Manager Relations

Having assumed responsibility for the property, it is vital that the manager maintain a mutually satisfactory relationship with the owner. To avoid confusion, from this point on, only one member of the management firm should deal directly with the owner. The manager's ability to care for the property, coupled with the good will arising from personal contact with the owner, will build a lasting and mutually profitable business relationship.

Monthly Reports

The principal means of regular communication between the manager and the owner or owning corporation is the monthly earnings report. This report usually includes rental receipts, miscellaneous income, gross income, an itemized list of all disbursements and operating expenses, total expenses for the month, cash on hand at the beginning of the month, amount forwarded to the principal (owner), and cash balance on hand. The manager also should submit a list of delinquent accounts and inform the owner of lawsuits or other events pertaining to the property.

The manager can demonstrate continuing personal interest in the property by always including a cover letter along with the financial report. Above all, the monthly report should be honest and intelligent to assure the owner that the manager understands how all the variables interact to affect the revenue from the property.

Personal Contact

Personal contact with the owner can be made by a short visit or a telephone call. Letters or e-mail can be used to reach an owner who is out of town and to confirm decisions already reached through personal discussions or telephone conversations.

Ongoing Contact

The frequency with which the manager should contact the owner is dictated by the urgency of the circumstances and by the owner's personal preference. Some owners hire management firms for the sole purpose of relieving themselves of all duties and decisions arising from property ownership. Other owners only want to avoid the burden of soliciting rentals, collecting rents, handling tenant complaints, and other daily management functions, but wish to be included in all other concerns of property ownership.

The manager must know what kind and frequency of communication the owner wants, what types of information are important to what owners, and to make sure that the owners are informed accordingly. Furthermore, the property manager must be able to deal effectively with a variety of personalities and temperaments. Different degrees of tactfulness or bluntness are required for different types of people, and maintaining a productive working relationship requires the ability to tell when each is to be used or avoided.

case study

Doug Conners, CPM, is the owner of an accredited management organization, which manages property for individuals, pension funds, and trusts. He started his property management career as an employee of a company that managed investment properties for a large number of owners. The owner of this company was a dynamic individual who had built up the business over many years.

When the owner died, however, succeeding managers failed to maintain good relationships with the client property owners. After losing many clients, the company was forced to close. One disgruntled ex-client, for whom Doug had been the principal manager, encouraged him to set up his own company and subsequently transferred its holdings for him to manage.

Case Study Review

1. Which approach should Doug take to avoid the mistakes of the previous managers?

    a. Devote time to maintaining sound owner relations

    b. Hire new maintenance personnel at the time of takeover

    c. Hire competent leasing agents

    d. Make sure that the security deposits are properly accounted for

2. As Doug's company grows and he acquires more properties to manage, he can

    a. relax because obviously he has a good reputation.

    b. form a transitional team that will develop expertise to oversee the acquisition of a new property.

    c. expect staff to report to him daily so that he is aware of any problems.

    d. turn the accounting and financial reporting to the bookkeeper.

■ Summary

A property owner and manager may enter into one of three relationships: employer-employee, principal-agent, or trustor-trustee. A principal-agent relationship is created with a written property management contract signed by both parties. Certain legal and ethical considerations due to the owner from the manager are implicit in this agency relationship. As agent for the owner, the manager must be loyal and pledge to act in the best interest of the principal and to handle all transactions in regard to the property with honesty and discretion.

The term of a management contract varies with the size of the property, the manager's responsibilities, and the future intentions of the parties. Any properly drawn contract will outline the responsibilities of the property manager and those of the owner.

The contract should clearly state the amount of the fee, when it is to be paid, and in what manner. Independent agent managers may charge a flat fee or a percentage of gross collectible income. Sometimes an additional fee is paid to the manager for his or her leasing activities.

The transfer of responsibilities for the property should take place as soon as possible after the contract between the owner and manager has been signed. The owner must provide all relevant and necessary information to the manager. Special attention should be paid to the transfer of security deposits, which are often regulated by state law.

■ Review Questions

True-False

1. In a principal-agent relationship, the property manager is usually a general agent of the owner.
   a. True
   b. False

2. If the principal asks the manager to violate the law, the agent must do so under the fiduciary duty of obedience.
   a. True
   b. False

3. A property manager may commingle client funds with the regular office funds.
   a. True
   b. False

4. A percentage fee is often disadvantageous to the property manager.
   a. True
   b. False

5. A gratuitous agent can be held liable for negligence, even though no compensation is paid for his or her services.
   a. True
   b. False

6. The Uniform Property Management Compensation Rate recommended by BOMA is a valuable standard for the property manager to use in negotiating a fee structure.
   a. True
   b. False

7. The information required for an efficient takeover of a property includes utility account numbers, apartment sizes, and the number of currently vacant units.
   a. True
   b. False

8. A personal walk-through inspection should always be part of a takeover process.
   a. True
   b. False

9. Tenant security deposit balances and accounting are an essential part of the takeover process.
   a. True
   b. False

10. The frequency with which a manager should personally contact the owner is determined by the manager's preferences and style of operation.
   a. True
   b. False

Multiple-Choice

1. The law of agency requires the manager to
   a. deposit the property's tenant funds in the manager's business account.
   b. maintain confidentiality and loyalty to the owner's best interests.
   c. obey the owner's every instruction, even if that requires unethical behavior.
   d. act with self-interest in managing the property.

2. The principal-agent relationship in property management is created by
   a. management contract.
   b. listing agreement.
   c. employment contract.
   d. equitable title.

3. A bank employee is asked to manage the properties owned by the bank. At the very least, the employee should be given
   a. a power of attorney.
   b. written authorization to sign leases.
   c. a management contract.
   d. permission to evict tenants.

4. A property manager who is authorized to obligate his or her principal in a contractual manner is a
   a. trustee.
   b. trustor.
   c. special agent.
   d. general agent.

5. The relationship that a property manager who is an agent has with the owner who is a principal is
   a. confidential.
   b. ethical.
   c. fiduciary.
   d. a power of attorney.

6. Under what circumstances may an agent terminate the management contract early and not be subject to a claim for damages by the owner?
   a. If the tenants request that the agent be replaced
   b. If the agent takes a personal dislike to the owner or some member of the owner's staff
   c. If the owner causes the agent damages or liability by violating a law
   d. If the management contract becomes unprofitable because of high vacancies

7. When revenue is low in a certain month, the management agreement will usually provide that the manager
   a. advance funds to cover the deficit.
   b. petition the owner to make up the deficit.
   c. stave off creditors until the next rental payments come in.
   d. pay costs from a reserve fund established previously.

8. Mixing owners' funds with personal funds is an illegal activity called
   a. redlining.
   b. commingling.
   c. steering.
   d. conversion.

9. How are management fees determined?
   a. Agreement of participating property managers
   b. Average of local rates charged
   c. Set by state law
   d. Negotiated between the parties

10. Which type of fee is a wonderful incentive when the owner wants the manager to generate more income?
    a. Per-unit fee
    b. Flat fee
    c. Percentage fee
    d. Cost plus fee

11. To ensure a smooth takeover of a property, all of the following should be done *EXCEPT* the
    a. owner should provide all the necessary documents.
    b. manager should use a takeover checklist.
    c. manager should personally inspect the entire property.
    d. owner should offer the tenants an opportunity to terminate their leases.

12. Security deposit balances and accounting are an essential part of a property takeover. How should the new property manager handle security deposits?
    a. Follow the owner's instructions
    b. Handle the deposits in the same manner as the previous manager
    c. Adhere to state laws
    d. Create a new system

13. To maintain an ongoing satisfactory relationship with the owner, the manager should
    a. send the owner reports only on written request from the owner.
    b. send monthly earnings reports and a personal letter.
    c. contact the owner only in an emergency.
    d. send quarterly written reports and monthly phone calls.

14. A flat-fee arrangement would be most appropriate when managing a(n)
    a. superregional mall.
    b. condominium community.
    c. office complex.
    d. retail store.

15. A property manager had to begin an eviction action for one of the tenants. This kind of information
    a. should be given to the owner annually.
    b. should be given to the owner on a monthly basis, at least.
    c. is evidence of a breach of the manager's fiduciary duties.
    d. is bad news and should always be delivered in person.

chapter three

Economics and Planning

■ Key Terms

cash flow

comparative income and
  expense analysis

contraction

expansion

five-year forecast

gross collectible rental
  income

management plan

market

market analysis

operating budget

operating costs

optimum rents

property analysis

recession

reserve funds

revival

supply and demand

learning objectives

On completing this chapter, you will be able to

■ list four types of changes in the general economy that affect the real estate market;

■ name and explain the four business cycles in the economy (expansion, recession, contraction, and revival);

■ identify the key components of a management plan that reconciles the data collected from regional, neighborhood, and property analyses;

■ recognize the importance of the owner's objectives when formulating the management plan;

■ discuss the difference between an operating budget and a five-year forecast, and the value of each; and

■ explain how a comparative income and expense analysis can benefit the owner when making a decision for any major capital expenditure for repairs, alterations, or improvements.

■ Economics and Planning

Since the 1930s, the real estate market has been recognized as a key component of the general economy. Although much attention is given to real estate sales, rentals are just as important to the economy and are equally affected by local, state, and national economic trends. In order to assist owners, property managers must be able to assess the current and future potential of a particular property in order to develop a management plan for it.

A competent, professional management plan begins with a regional and neighborhood analysis, a thorough look at the potential rental income and expenses of the subject property, and a plan to help the owners reach their short-term and long-term goals. The management plan becomes a blueprint; its implementation provides direction for the property manager and the basis for evaluation by the owners.

The General Business Economy

A **market** is defined as an exchange of goods and services between willing sellers and willing buyers. For example, the *real estate market* refers to the activity of buyers and sellers of real estate. There is no single real estate market; rather, the real estate market is made up of the scattered, unrelated transactions that occur between property buyers and sellers and landlords and tenants.

The complex marketplace responds to different factors, especially the principle of **supply and demand**. When the supply of a product is less than the demand for it, its price will increase; and when the supply of a product is greater than the demand for it, its price will decrease. In a perfect economy, the forces of supply and demand are always seeking to balance each other (a condition referred to by economists as *equilibrium*), which creates a stable economy. In reality, supply and demand are rarely balanced.

Other events in the market also cause ripples in the market. These tend to fall into four categories: seasonal variations, cyclic fluctuations, long-term movements, and random changes.

Seasonal variations. Seasonal variations occur at regular intervals at least once a year and arise from nature and custom. For example, a nine-month school year has seasonal impact on rentals in college and university towns. Retirees swell the wintertime populations of many southern cities. These changes are predictable, and property managers can be prepared to make any necessary adjustments to counter economic shifts.

Cyclic fluctuations. Historically, economists have concentrated on cyclic fluctuations in the general economy. Business cycles are usually defined as wavelike movements of increasing and decreasing economic prosperity. A cycle consists of four phases:

1. **Expansion** (in which the economy grows)
2. **Recession** (in which growth slows)
3. **Contraction** (in which economic activity decreases)
4. **Revival** (in which the expansion begins again)

Although business cycles technically consist of these four phases, most discussions deal simply with expansion and contraction. Business cycles are recurrent but not periodic; that is, they vary in duration and timing. Through empirical research, economists have observed cycles in the general economy that vary from 1 to 12 years in length. (See Figure 3.1.)

Long-term movements. Long-term movements of the general economy, usually measured over 50 years or more, reflect the overall direction the economy is taking. Such movements are believed to result from population growth and shifts, technological breakthroughs, the rate of savings and investment, and use of natural resources. Long-term movements in the real estate industry are often shorter—sometimes only five to ten years—because real estate activities occur at local levels at irregular intervals. They do follow the same basic pattern whenever a new land area is developed or an existing area redeveloped.

Random changes. Nonperiodic fluctuations of the economy may be caused by legislative and judicial decisions or by strikes, hurricanes, wars, fires, storms, floods, and other catastrophes. These changes, impossible to predict or analyze, may affect one or more sectors of the aggregate economy or all industries in an area or one industry nationwide. Real estate activity, especially construction, is particularly vulnerable to labor strikes, political changes, and natural disasters.

Government influences. The government attempts to control major economic fluctuations by setting up a number of programs and regulatory agencies to buffer the effect of a severe economic downturn. Such programs include Social Security, welfare, Medicare, and unemployment benefits. Regulatory agencies, including the Federal Reserve Board, enact policies that seek to control runaway growth.

Indirect government actions also have significant impact on business cycles. Such actions can include changes to tax rates, affordable housing programs, and the general spending and debt financing policies of the government. For example, when the government decreases taxes, people have more money to save or spend, and the general economy is expected to heat up as a result.

Figure 3.1 | The Business Cycle

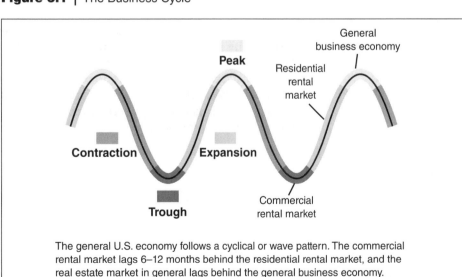

The general U.S. economy follows a cyclical or wave pattern. The commercial rental market lags 6–12 months behind the residential rental market, and the real estate market in general lags behind the general business economy. For instance, if the general business economy is at a "peak", the residential rental market may be in a growth or "expansion" mode, while the commercial rental market may be depressed or in a "trough".

The Real Estate Economy

A downturn in the general business economy means that fewer people can afford to buy real estate, which then decreases the demand for real estate in relation to the supply of real estate. When people cannot afford to buy, there is a greater demand for rental housing.

Since 2000, interest rates dropped to near record lows, fueling an incredible demand for buying real estate. However, that bubble burst in 2007 when interest rates began to climb and many adjustable-rate mortgages reset to levels that a great deal of homeowners could not afford. Today, many houses stand empty, creating a demand for rental housing. In late 2007, many areas of the country were reporting 90 to 95 percent occupancy of rental units as well as increasing rental rates.

Local population trends also affect the value of real estate. A large influx of people into a community (because of increased job opportunities, for example) will cause the value of real estate to go up. A decrease in population will have the opposite effect. The demographics of that population will also affect real estate values. For example, an increase in retirement-age citizens will increase the value of certain types of properties (retirement communities) while decreasing the value of other types of properties (large, high-maintenance single-family homes).

The rental market.   Any changes in the supply of and demand for residential, commercial, and industrial properties have implications for the property manager. When the economy is heating up, the rental market for property is generally good and vacancies are low. More rentable space is built as properties continue to offer attractive returns to investors.

As the cycle peaks, the supply of space that can be occupied equals and then often exceeds the demand. At this point, rents fall and vacancy rates increase. During the contraction phase, the rental market is poor, vacancy rates are high, and property owners must compete for tenants. The result is a drastic reduction in rents. As the cycle reaches the trough, the demand for space once again equals and begins to surpass the supply of available space, so rental rates as well as construction starts begin to increase.

Specific cycles in the residential rental market correspond roughly to cycles in multifamily residential housing starts. The rental market for commercial property lags from six months to one year behind residential rental market trends because commercial leases generally are longer and require more time to reflect current conditions. Because the real estate market lags behind the general economy in the short cycle, the general business economy often predicts trends that eventually affect the real estate market.

> ### *Liability Alert!*
>
> #### Anticipate Change to Avoid Financial Loss
>
> Property managers who analyze the real estate market and recognize trends can be prepared for economic fluctuations and crises. By anticipating changes in the market and adjusting rentals and other factors within their control, property managers can minimize the effect of contractions in the real estate cycle and keep their vacancy rates as low as possible. Tracking economic trends and specific cycles in the real estate sector provides a background against which to view the specific conditions and characteristics of each property. The ability to anticipate economic trends and market behavior provides the property manager with excellent insulation against owner dissatisfaction.

■ The Management Plan

The basic blueprint of a property manager's responsibilities is the management plan. A **management plan** is the financial and operational strategy for the ongoing management of a property. The plan is based on three basic factors:

1. Regional and neighborhood market analysis
2. Analysis of the subject property itself
3. Analysis and application of the owner's objectives for the property

On the basis of these three factors, the manager should be able to draw up a management plan and a budget that are feasible in terms of both present and future business and real estate economic cycles. Critical market indicators are occupancy and absorption rates and new starts. The management plan will include a market analysis, an alternative analysis, and proposed financing, as well as conclusions and recommendations.

> ### *Liability Alert!*
>
> #### Get It in Writing
>
> Because of the time and effort involved in creating a management plan, the manager should not undertake this task unless he or she is to receive adequate compensation or has already signed a contract. However, competitive pressures may force property management firms to complete a plan as part of the bidding process, for which they may or may not be compensated.

■ Market Analysis

A comprehensive **market analysis** integrates information about the larger overall region with detailed information about the specific, local area where the property is located. Whatever the case may be, all real property is part of the national real estate economy and is subject to the same cyclic trends. It is the responsibility of the property manager to identify major economic trends and their effect on the value of a specific property at his or her particular market level.

Regional Market Analysis

A regional market analysis should include demographic and economic information on the regional or metropolitan area in which the subject property is located. The regional analysis typically presents population statistics and trends, a list of major employers in the area, income and employment data, a description of transportation facilities, and supply and demand trends. It also should explore the economic base of the city and prospects for the future in that locale.

Neighborhood Market Analysis

Generally, property management is carried out at the local level. Before the manager can determine the optimum income that can be realized from a building, he or she must first determine the economic climate of the neighborhood real estate market.

Neighborhood analysis should begin with a tour of the area. Equipped with local maps, area zoning ordinances, applicable building codes, and statistical data on the population, the property manager should assess six major factors in the neighborhood market area:

1. **Boundaries.** A neighborhood usually is defined as an area within which common characteristics of population and land use prevail. In the absence of any obvious boundaries, the manager must determine how much land is under common use and shares a similar population.

2. **Local building codes and regulations.** While establishing a neighborhood's boundaries, the property manager should take note of growth-restricting features such as rivers, parks, highways, and railroad tracks. Zoning variances and restrictions should also be noted because zoning may encourage or inhibit expansion or the variety of uses available for a particular property.

3. **Transportation and utilities.** Transportation facilities are often crucial.

   Many apartment dwellers desire proximity to public transportation, as do employees in office buildings. Access to and from major streets, traffic patterns, and the traffic count in a neighborhood are of concern to commercial ventures such as strip centers or shopping malls. Industrial enterprises must have access to transportation facilities to distribute their goods, so rail heads, major highways, and airports are important to industrial tenants.

   The cost and quality of utility services will also affect the desirability of any type of real property. Residential and commercial buildings must offer certain basic amenities—electricity, gas, water, heat, and air-conditioning—to attract individual and corporate tenants. Industrial users will be particularly concerned with heavy-duty power lines, sprinklers, separate sewerage systems, and other unique utility services.

4. **Economy.** A neighborhood that has a diverse business sector is in better economic condition than an area that depends on a single major industry for its support. The property manager can draw on several sources of statistical information for help in assessing the economic health of a neighborhood. Brokers, appraisers, and local newspapers are fruitful sources, as is the local chamber of commerce, which should be able to supply data on the number and type of businesses in the area, the volume of their activity, and the general trend of growth in the past and for the future. Rental rates currently being charged in the neighborhood are another sound indicator of the present economic strength of the real estate market.

5. **Supply and demand.** The occupancy rate for a particular type of property reflects the relationship between supply and demand for that type of space at its current rental level. Occupancy and vacancy rates continually fluctuate, reflecting supply and demand. A high occupancy rate indicates a shortage of space and the possibility of rental increases. A low rate will result in tenant demands for lower rents or other concessions as the tenants negotiate from a position of market strength.

6. **Neighborhood amenities and facilities.** The final checkpoint in the manager's survey of a neighborhood is more relevant to residential property managers than to managers of commercial or industrial real estate. Nonetheless, any amenities that make the neighborhood attractive to potential residents will indirectly benefit business and industry by providing a local pool of potential consumers and employees. When touring the neighborhood, the manager should note the number and location of parks, playgrounds, theaters, restaurants, schools, colleges, places of worship, and any other social or cultural organizations that will be attractive to potential tenants.

Evaluating the Data

Once the regional and neighborhood market surveys are complete, the manager can begin to analyze the information. The analyses are as reliable as the judgments behind them. Only a manager who is knowledgeable about real estate economic cycles can begin to assess their impact on future trends in his or her own market.

By reconciling the data, the manager can arrive at the **optimum rent** for a standard unit of that type of property within the market area. From this figure, the expected base income for the property can be calculated.

■ Property Analysis

While the market analysis determines the optimum rental for standard space in the area, a **property analysis,** on the other hand, familiarizes the manager with the nature and condition of a particular building and with its position relative to similar properties in the neighborhood. The owner will need this analysis in order to make an informed decision before making any financial decisions.

A useful property analysis includes a thorough description of the subject property, data on similar properties in the area, data to be able to estimate the average operating cost of the building, and suggestions as to what is needed to make the subject property competitive to the best available space. The owner needs all of this information in order to make an informed decision before making any financial decisions.

Leases

When taking over a new property, the manager should begin by reading all leases and any other information in the file. The terms of each lease will disclose the amount and durability of rental income. To avoid any surprises, the manager should be alert for concessions, renewal options, and termination notices. If the property was built prior to 1978, the residential manager must look for the lead-based paint disclosure forms that should be in every tenant's file.

Vacancy and loss rates can show whether previous management was efficient. If leases have a low renewal rate (high tenant turnover), the quality of tenant services may be poor or the rental rate may be too high for the market. If there is no turnover, possibly the rents are too low, and there may be an opportunity to raise rents. Summarizing this information on a spreadsheet can assist the manager in organizing the material to provide a methodical analysis.

Physical Condition of the Premises

A thorough inspection of the building's exterior, common interior areas, and equipment should provide the property manager with the additional data necessary to calculate maintenance and operating costs for the upcoming year.

Exterior appearance.   The exterior inspection should begin with the overall outward appearance of the structure, including its age and style as well as the condition of its walkways and landscaping. All common areas should be scrutinized for evidence of deferred maintenance. If the building does not present as pleasing a facade as others in the area, the manager can suggest corrective measures to improve the initial presentation of the premises.

Interior space.   Inside the building, the manager determines the total amount of usable space or number of individual rental units in the building. The ability of a space to command optimum rents for the area depends not only on the desirability of its design but also on the quality of its fixtures and amenities. Whether the space is commercial, industrial, or residential, the condition of the hardware, plumbing, walls, and electrical fixtures should be carefully noted.

Equipment.   The condition of the hardware, plumbing, walls, and electrical fixtures must be considered whether the space is commercial, industrial, or residential. The manager's tour of the building's machinery, equipment, and amenities will disclose their condition and age, need for major repairs, and the amount of personnel and supplies required to keep them operating efficiently.

> "You don't get a second chance to make a first impression" is especially true in property management. Prospective tenants form their initial impressions of the premises based on "curb appeal," what they see as they approach the building.

Liability Alert!

Watch for Health and Safety Hazards

While reviewing the physical inventory, the manager should look for areas of deferred maintenance and curable obsolescence. The tour of the building should show compliance with building codes.

If the manager suspects that any portion of the property contains a contaminant or safety hazard, he or she should raise the issue with the owner and require a professional inspection and/or a complete cleanup before agreeing to manage the property. Insurance companies or the local fire marshal will usually conduct a safety and fire inspection at no charge.

Evaluation through Comparables

The evaluation of comparable properties (comparables) provides insight into the competition faced by the manager's property. Things to consider include building size, rental rates, vacancy rates, location, construction, age, special features and amenities, the condition of the premises, the size of the building staff, and, if possible, operating expenses for comparable premises. Industry standards obtained from professional property management associations are also valuable.

Operating costs.   All of the following information gives the manager a good idea of the routine **operating costs** over the course of the year: salaries for the building staff; cost of utilities not charged to the tenants; contract services, such as lawn or elevator maintenance, rubbish removal, and security guards; supplies and equipment; and administrative expenses for advertising and management.

The manager can now begin to develop both a rental schedule and an operating budget for the subject property's management plan, identifying and estimating expenditures needed to yield a net return that is in accord with the owner's objectives. Additionally, the owner should be advised of any estimates of any capital expenditures that may be required to make the building competitive with similar properties in the neighborhood, if that is consistent with the owner's goals. Finally, the manager can assist the owner by setting priorities for the proposed tasks.

■ Analysis of the Owner's Objectives

The management plan cannot be completed until the manager has identified and analyzed the owner's goals, which will vary widely among the individual, corporate, fiduciary, and government owners. The management plan may suggest changing the current operation of the property through rehabilitation, alteration, and modernization. Regardless, the owner's objectives will be the deciding factor in the adoption of the management plan. If the manager cannot successfully execute a particular plan as outlined by the owner, the two should try to renegotiate it.

Most institutional and corporate investors have well-defined, written goals in the form of policy statements or investment guidelines. On the other hand, few individual owners have developed long-range plans. A property manager can make a real contribution by assisting the owner to commit to establishing a set of written goals.

■ Preparing the Management Plan

The steps usually taken in the preparation of the management plan include:

1. Operating budget (usually for one year)
2. Five-year forecast
3. Comparative income and expense analysis

To formulate the financial planning reports, the following information must be determined:

- **Optimum rents.** The ideal rent for a specific type of unit in a defined market area that may need to be adjusted to reflect specific advantages and disadvantages of the subject property.
- **Gross scheduled rental income.** The income determined by multiplying the amount of space in the building by the base rental rate for that type of space.
- **Total anticipated revenue.** The estimated revenue after deducting the percentage of probable rent loss resulting from vacancies, tenant defaults on leases, and tenant turnover. The resulting figure is the gross adjusted rental income, sometimes termed the **gross collectible rental income,** because it represents monies that may actually be collected after rent loss. Other income earned from a parking garage, vending machines, and laundry rooms should

be included. The sum of the gross collectible rental income and the additional income constitutes the manager's estimate of gross effective revenue during the upcoming year.

■ **Yearly operating costs.** The expense portion of the operating budget that projects realistic supportable estimates of operating costs for that particular property. These costs can include salaries, utilities, contract services, supplies, insurance, and more, and are usually based on the records for the previous year and/or on the analysis of the data obtained from neighborhood and property analyses.

■ **Necessary reserve funds.** In the expense category of the operating budget, **reserve funds** are monies set aside for replacement expenditures not covered by insurance, such as roof or furnace repairs, usually under maintenance or repairs. The amount varies depending on the condition and type of property.

■ **Cash flow in light of the owner's objectives. Cash flow** is the amount of money available for use after paying expenses and the debt service (the mortgage). It is determined by subtracting the total adjusted operating costs plus debt service from the anticipated revenue for the coming year. The operating budget may need to be modified if the annual cash flow does not reflect the cost of the property and the desired return on investment.

Operating Budget

Now the manager is ready to draw up a one-year projected **operating budget** for the property in its present condition, using all of the aforementioned data. See the sample budget for a three-story walkup apartment building consisting of 12 units shown in Figure 3.2. The rental rates are strictly for purposes of illustration and are not to be taken as typical of any locality.

Figure 3.2 | Annual Operating Budget

Income			
	3 studio @ $550	$19,800	
	6 one-bedroom @ $700/month	50,400	
	3 two-bedroom @ $850/month	30,600	
	Gross scheduled rental income less 5%	100,800	
	Vacancy and rent loss	− 5,000	
	Gross collectible rental income	95,800	
	Income from other sources	3,500	
	Total anticipated income		$99,300
Expenses			
	Real estate taxes	$11,900	
	Salaries	18,800	
	Utilities	5,200	
	Supplies	700	
	Maintenance and repairs	3,500	
	Insurance	1,500	
	Administrative	1,200	
	Management @ 6% of gross income	5,700	
	Reserves	1,300	
	Total budgeted expenses		$49,800
Net Operating Income before Debt Service			$49,500
Debt Service			
	$290,000 @ 8%	23,200	
Cash Flow			$26,300

Five-Year Forecast

A stronger picture of the property's income potential is a **five-year forecast,** a long-term projection of estimated expenditures and income based on predictable changes. The budget figures are arrived at by calculating and averaging all income and expenses for each of the next five years.

Before preparing a long-term forecast, the manager should study the market trends affecting all income and expense sources. Before setting the median income for the forecasted period, the manager must consider the current rate of rental increases in the area, the potential for growth or decline in the area, and rent increases stemming from any projected improvements to the property.

Property management professionals have a saying: "Unexpected expenditures may be expected." Roof repair, boiler replacement, outside masonry repair, and expenses due to flooding or other catastrophe not covered by insurance are only a few of the unforeseen contingencies that can arise. Also, many mortgage loans under federal government programs require establishing a reserve fund for replacement expenditures.

Liability Alert!

Make Realistic Projections

Depending on the general business economy during the next five years, operating costs will vary, quite possibly increasing at different estimated rates. These expenses must be realistically estimated based on observable trends. Major influences to consider include the rate of inflation, increases in the cost of labor and supplies, tax hikes, and rate increases in insurance premiums.

Comparative Income and Expense Analysis

The final component for the management plan is a **comparative income and expense analysis,** an estimate of the costs of improvements, alterations, or remodeling that are consistent with the owner's objectives and are needed to command optimum rentals. This analysis provides the owner with the potential income increase resulting from the proposed capital improvement and how long it will take to recoup the owner's initial capital expenditure.

Liability Alert!

Make Realistic Projections

The manager's estimates of capital expenditures must be based on accurate information on the costs of construction, materials, and labor involved for any proposed improvements. The manager must then compute the increase in rental income or decrease in expenses that will result from these improvements.

The cash flow generated after improvement should be compared with the return on investment for the property in its "as is" condition. With this analysis, the manager can demonstrate how long it will take to recoup the proposed capital. The comparative analysis also shows the estimated additional annual income or cash flow to be generated by the improvement.

Presenting the Plan

The plan should be thoroughly and neatly prepared, for many owners will judge a property manager's ability by the appearance and accuracy of submitted documents. In response, the owner may do any of the following:

■ Authorize all suggested repairs and alterations in an effort to increase long-term income or reduce taxes

Figure 3.3 | Five-Year Forecast

	Base Year	1st Year % Incr.	1st Year $ Amount	2nd Year % Incr.	2nd Year $ Amount	3rd Year % Incr.	3rd Year $ Amount	4th Year % Incr.	4th Year $ Amount	5th Year % Incr.	5th Year $ Amount
Income											
3 studio @ $550	$19,800	10.0%	$21,800	5.0%	$22,900	5.0%	$24,000	5.0%	$25,200	10.0%	$27,700
6 one-bedroom @ $700/month	50,400	10.0%	55,400	5.0%	58,200	5.0%	61,100	5.0%	64,200	10.0%	70,600
3 two-bedroom @ $850/month	30,600	10.0%	33,700	10.0%	37,100	5.0%	39,000	5.0%	41,000	10.0%	45,100
Gross scheduled rental income	100,800		110,900		118,200		124,100		130,400		143,400
Less 5% vacancy and rent loss	−5,000	0.0%	−5,500	0.0%	−5,900	0.0%	−6,200	0.0%	−6,500	0.0%	−7,200
Gross collectible rental income	95,800		105,400		112,300		117,900		123,900		136,200
Income from other sources	3,500	5.0%	3,700	5.0%	3,900	5.0%	4,100	5.0%	4,300	5.0%	4,500
Total anticipated income	99,300		109,100		116,200		122,000		128,200		140,700
Expenses											
Real estate taxes	11,900	7.0%	12,700	15.0%	14,600	5.0%	15,300	5.0%	16,100	5.0%	16,900
Salaries	18,800	4.0%	19,600	4.0%	20,400	4.0%	21,200	4.0%	22,000	4.0%	22,900
Utilities	5,200	8.0%	5,600	8.0%	6,000	8.0%	6,500	8.0%	7,000	8.0%	7,600
Supplies	700	10.0%	800	8.0%	900	10.0%	1,000	10.0%	1,100	10.0%	1,200
Maintenance and repairs	3,500	10.0%	3,900	5.0%	4,100	10.0%	4,500	8.0%	4,900	8.0%	5,300
Insurance	1,500	15.0%	1,700	10.0%	1,900	10.0%	2,100	10.0%	2,300	10.0%	2,500
Administrative	1,200	8.0%	1,300	8.0%	1,400	8.0%	1,500	8.0%	1,600	8.0%	1,700
Management @ 6% gross income	5,700	fixed 6.0%	6,300	fixed 6.0%	6,700	incr. to 6.5%	7,700	fixed 6.5%	8,100	fixed 6.5%	8,900
Reserves	1,300	10.0%	1,400	10.0%	1,500	10.0%	1,700	10.0%	1,900	10.0%	2,100
Total budged expenses	49,800		53,300		57,500		61,500		65,000		69,100
Net Operating Income before Debt Service	49,500		55,800		58,700		60,500		63,200		71,600
Debt Service $290,000 @ 8%	23,200	fixed	23,200	fixed	23,200	fixed	23,200	fixed	23,200	fixed	23,200
Cash Flow	$26,300		$32,600		$35,500		$37,300		$40,000		$48,400

Figure 3.4 | Comparative Income and Expense Analysis

	Property As Is	Property with Improvements
Income		
Rental	$41,000	$47,500
Other	2,000	4,000
Total	$43,000	$51,500
Expenses		
Real estate taxes	$5,000	$5,000
Salaries	8,500	8,500
Utilities	4,000	4,500
Supplies	500	500
Maintenance and repairs	1,500	1,500
Insurance	500	500
Administrative	200	200
Management @ 6% of gross income	2,500	3,000
Reserves	300	300
Total budgeted expenses	$23,000	$24,000
Net Operating Income before Debt Service	$20,000	$27,500
Debt Service		
$90,000 @ 10% constant	$9,000	$9,000
Cash Flow	$11,000	$18,500

Increase of $7,500 per year in cash flow. Initial investment of $15,000 to improve property will be returned within two years.

- Decide that only deferred maintenance should be performed to preserve the property's value without tying up additional working capital
- Make no changes at all, preferring to get as much income as possible from the property in the short term without making any capital expenditures

case study

After graduating from college with honors and earning a master's degree in economics, Charles Gill was hired by the local urban renewal authority in his home town of approximately 500,000 people. His responsibilities were in the areas of statistics, financial planning, and research. When activities of the urban renewal authority began to wind down on completion of a major downtown redevelopment project, one of the directors, a businessman who had acquired some real estate investment property, hired Charles to manage one of his residential rental properties.

The local economy had slowed with the general national recession, and real estate prices were severely depressed in many areas, including Charles's town. To make matters worse, a local factory that built appliances had closed, creating widespread unemployment. Charles saw there were suddenly many properties available that were priced far less than they had sold for just a few years before. He also saw that although the rental market was not booming, tenants were shifting to buildings with lower rent.

Case Study Review

1. Which information is important for Charles to note when preparing a management plan for his new employer?

    a. People are hesitant to relocate.

    b. Properties are rising in value.

    c. Tenants are relocating.

    d. The economy is booming.

2. What is the effect of the shutdown of the local factory that built appliances?

    a. Housing prices should rise.

    b. Demand for rentals increases.

    c. Employment is booming.

    d. The economy is booming.

■ Summary

The business economy moves in long-term cycles affecting the real estate market. During one full cycle, business activity progresses from a peak period, in which demand exceeds 35, to a time of depressed transaction, in which supply exceeds demand, and then gradually back to peak performance.

Owners of real property cannot reduce the amount of leasable space in their buildings when demand falls and vacancy rates rise. A manager who can analyze the real estate market, recognize trends, and anticipate their effects can hopefully shield the property from the impact of economic cycles.

The property manager must integrate specific studies (regional analysis, neighborhood analysis, and a property analysis) and then reconcile the data collected to formulate a management proposal. The manager develops the management plan based on the available capital resources and the income requirements of the owner.

After drawing up an operating budget for the property, as is, for the coming year, the manager makes up a five-year forecast that draws on every available resource to anticipate future market trends in the area and to estimate increases in both operating costs and rental income. The forecast should demonstrate future cash flow benefits to the owner.

Any recommendations for major capital expenditures should include a comparative income and expense analysis showing the potential increase in income. The analysis should project how long it will take to recoup the owner's initial capital expenditure.

The objectives of the property owner determine what action is eventually taken on the management plan. Depending on their situation, owners can be profit oriented, be interested in tax benefits, maintain the status quo, and have other objectives.

■ Review Questions

True-False

1. Economic changes that occur at regular, annual intervals are called *cyclic fluctuations.*
   a. True
   b. False

2. A business cycle consists of four phases: expansion, recession, contraction, and revival.
   a. True
   b. False

3. Long-term economic movements are usually measured over terms of at least 50 years.
   a. True
   b. False

4. Property managers need to have a clear understanding of their own area of expertise but do not need to understand broad principles of economics.
   a. True
   b. False

5. A management plan is composed of three elements: a regional analysis, a neighborhood analysis, and an analysis of the subject property.
   a. True
   b. False

6. Zoning ordinances and building codes would be helpful in performing a regional market analysis.
   a. True
   b. False

7. Property analysis begins with a study of the terms of each tenant's lease.
   a. True
   b. False

8. A building's exterior appearance is not an especially important part of a property analysis, which should concentrate on more financially significant elements of the property.
   a. True
   b. False

9. Antitrust considerations prohibit a property manager from consulting property management associations for industry standards for various types of properties available in preparing an evaluation based on comparables.
   a. True
   b. False

10. The owner's objectives are relevant to the preparation of a management plan.
   a. True
   b. False

Multiple-Choice

1. Which *BEST* describes a market?
   a. Expansion and contraction phases
   b. Seasonal variations
   c. Cyclic and random changes
   d. Exchange of goods between buyers and sellers

2. The four phases of the business cycle are
   a. inflation, expansion, growth, and contraction.
   b. expansion, growth, contraction, and revival.
   c. expansion, recession, contraction, and revival.
   d. contraction, growth, revival, and contraction.

3. Which is considered a random change that affects the economy?
   a. Nine-month college schedules
   b. Winter storms
   c. Hurricane Katrina
   d. Outsourcing of jobs

4. Which would be one of the more indirect government actions to influence the economy?
   a. Government decreasing taxes
   b. Downturn in general business economy
   c. Closure of defense facilities
   d. Major plant closing

5. The residential rental market corresponds roughly to
   a. cycles in multifamily housing starts.
   b. commercial properties.
   c. industrial property.
   d. construction of new shopping centers.

6. The financial and operational strategy for the ongoing management of a property is the
   a. property manager.
   b. evaluation of all properties in the area.
   c. management plan.
   d. five-year forecast.

7. A property manager can measure economic trends through all of the following *EXCEPT*
   a. a regional market analysis.
   b. a neighborhood market analysis.
   c. supply and demand.
   d. an operating budget.

8. In the operating budget, the expenditure that accounts for money for replacement expenditures is called
   a. cash flow.
   b. reserve funds.
   c. variable expenses.
   d. direct costs.

9. The income determined by multiplying the amount of space by the base rent for that class of space, equals the
   a. total anticipated revenue.
   b. operating costs.
   c. gross scheduled rental income.
   d. reserve funds.

10. Anticipated revenue minus total adjusted operating costs and debt service equals
    a. reserve funds.
    b. cash flow.
    c. the five-year forecast.
    d. variable expenses.

11. Which is the first step when preparing financial planning reports?
    a. Prepare five-year forecast
    b. Prepare an operating budget
    c. Establish optimum rents
    d. Predict anticipated revenue

12. The objective in a market analysis is to
    a. identify all properties comparable to the subject property.
    b. determine the average rate for comparable rental units.
    c. establish vacancy rates for comparable property.
    d. determine the optimum rental price for a standard space in the area.

13. To avoid any surprises when taking over a new property, the manager should first
    a. have a third party audit the books.
    b. hire a building engineer to evaluate the structure.
    c. review the insurance policies.
    d. read all the leases.

14. Prospective tenants form their initial impression of a rental property based on the
    a. personality of the manager or leasing agent.
    b. curb appeal of the property.
    c. appearance of the manager's office or quarters.
    d. inspection of the interior of the building.

15. The determining factor in the acceptance or rejection of the management plan will be the
    a. property analysis.
    b. owner's objectives.
    c. neighborhood analysis.
    d. five-year forecast.

chapter four

Leases and Tenant Issues

■ Key Terms

assignment	gross lease	security deposit
constructive eviction	index lease	statute of frauds
escalation clause	lease	step-up clause
estate for years	leasehold estate	subletting
estate from period to period	net lease	tenancy at sufferance
	percentage lease	tenancy at will

learning objectives

On completing this chapter, you will be able to

■ list and define four kinds of leasehold estates;

■ distinguish among the types of residential and commercial leases and describe the characteristics and uses of each;

■ explain how to protect the owner financially in a very long lease;

■ discuss three methods of maintaining effective, ongoing communication with the tenants;

■ describe the value of requiring maintenance forms in writing and dealing with tenants with excessive requests;

■ outline the fundamental components of a typical residential lease and the rights and responsibilities of both the lessor and lessee; and

■ understand the importance of state and local law in governing landlord-tenant relations.

The management contract formalizes the relationship between the property owner and the manager and specifies the rights and duties of each party. The **lease** sets up the rights and obligations of the landlord (owner/manager) and the tenant. The foundation for good landlord-tenant relations begins with a clearly written lease, clear understanding of the rules and regulations, and the establishment of a good communication system with tenants.

This chapter first details the estates and tenancies created by the lease as well as ways that rents are determined. The second part of the chapter discusses the importance of maintaining good relations with tenants. Effective managers know that dissatisfied tenants eventually vacate the property, and a high tenant turnover means greater expense for the owner in terms of advertising, redecorating, and uncollected rents.

Depending on the terms of the management contract, the property manger usually has responsibility for leasing the premises. Although the attorneys for the parties to the lease are responsible for its legal and technical details, property managers should be familiar with leasehold estates and basic lease clauses.

Liability Alert!

Be Aware of Landlord-Tenant Laws

All states and some cities have various laws regulating leases and the landlord-tenant relationship. Property managers must have a thorough understanding of those laws affecting the jurisdictions in which they operate. Historically, leases favored the lessor because of the superior bargaining position of the landlord, and the fact that attorneys representing the property owners and managers usually drafted the leases. This is changing, though, with revised legislation and judicial interpretation favoring the tenant.

■ Leasehold Estates

A **leasehold estate** is of limited duration and is created when an owner or a property manager (acting as the owner's agent) grants a tenant the right to occupy the owner's property for a specified period of time in exchange for some form of consideration. Leases are contracts, and contract rights are considered personal property rights. Either the landlord or tenant may transfer rights unless there is language in the contract that specifically prohibits such transfers. While the rights may be transferred, obligations usually remain with the original party, unless the obligations may be assumed by the new party. Although significant differences existed in the past, today the terms *estate* and *tenancy* are generally used interchangeably.

Liability Alert!

Know What the Lease Offers and Does Not Offer

Most leases will include a clause stipulating that the tenant cannot sell, assign, or pledge the leasehold interest without prior written approval of the property owner. For example, when an owner sells a leased-up apartment building, the new owner acquires not only the building but also the rights and obligations of the leases.

The following discussion of leasehold estates is based on common law characteristics. Property managers must consult state statutes for local law.

Estate for Years

An **estate** (or tenancy) **for years** is actually a misnomer. This tenancy is characterized as having a definite beginning and a definite end, which can be as little as a week or as long as 99 years—or even longer. At the end of the lease, neither party is required to give notice that the lease is over; the tenant surrenders the property to the landlord.

As estate for years is not terminated by the sale of the property or by the death of either the tenant or the landlord. If either dies, the rights and obligations continue to their heirs.

Liability Alert!

Termination Notice

Because an estate for years has a definite end, if the landlord wants notice that the tenant is planning to leave at the end of the term, the lease must contain a clause requiring the notice within a stated period. Although some states recognize an enforceable oral lease for less than a year, the prudent manager will put such agreements in writing.

Estate from Period to Period

An **estate from period to period,** or a periodic lease, is one that automatically renews unless either party gives notice of termination. These leases run week to week, month to month, or year to year. Notice is often equal to the period, but the time of notice may vary from a minimum of one week to a maximum of six months prior to termination. This estate may be created either by agreement or by operation of law.

Operation of law. A periodic estate arises when a tenant has possession of the property and pays rent under an invalid lease or a lease that does not specify the duration of the tenancy. A holdover tenancy is created when the tenant holding an estate for years remains in possession of the premises after the expiration of the lease. Acceptance of rental payments by the owner or property manager is considered legal proof of the owner's acquiescence to the holdover tenancy.

Tenancy at Will

Tenancy at will gives a tenant the right of possession with the consent of the owner for an indefinite period of time. This estate, like an estate from period to period, may be created either by express agreement or by operation of law. It exists only as long as both parties wish the estate to continue. An estate at will is terminated by the death of either party.

Liability Alert!

Notice for Tenancy at Will

In the past, an estate at will could be terminated without notice, but most states now require the party who wishes to terminate the tenancy to give some advance written notice. Property managers should consult their state statutes for the rights and obligations involved in tenancy at will.

Tenancy at Sufferance

Tenancy at sufferance occurs when a tenant obtains possession of the premises legally but then remains on the property without the owner's consent after the leasehold interest has expired. This tenant has no right to possession. The owner or property manager may either evict the tenant without notice or acquiesce to the tenancy.

> ### Liability Alert!
> #### Avoid Tenancies at Sufferance
>
> The owner's acceptance of rent payments constitutes acquiescence and creates an estate at will or an estate from period to period. This is a complex issue, and the property manager can avoid cost costly legal entanglements by ensuring that the written leases conform to local laws and statutes.

■ Types of Lease Payments

The three basic lease forms the property manager will be expected to administer are the gross lease, the net lease, and the percentage lease. The three types are differentiated by the manner in which rental compensation is computed and paid.

Gross Lease

Under a **gross lease,** sometimes called a straight lease, the tenant pays a fixed rental amount and the owner pays all other expenses for the property. Utility charges are generally paid by the tenant but may be negotiated between the parties. Most residential leases are gross leases.

Net Leases

Under a **net lease,** the tenant pays some or all of the expenses of the property in addition to the stated rent. Depending on the lease, tenants are obligated to pay utilities, real estate taxes, and other special assessments levied against the property, insurance premiums, and agreed-on items of repair and maintenance.

> ### Liability Alert!
> #### Triple-Net Leases Must Be Specific
>
> As property usage becomes more specialized, triple-net leases are more widely used, especially for industrial properties. The differences between a net lease and a triple-net lease are a matter of degree; that is, how many extra expenses the tenant is required to pay. The property manager should be explicit about the expenses for which the tenant is responsible.

Percentage Lease

The **percentage lease** is commonly used for retail property, especially malls. It usually provides for the payment of a fixed-base rental fee plus a percentage of the tenant's gross income in excess of a predetermined minimum amount of sales.

Although percentage payments may be prorated or paid monthly, payments are usually based on an annual computation.

■ Essential Provisions of a Valid Lease

Because a lease is a contract, the general requirements for a valid lease are similar to those for a legally enforceable contract. Both parties to the lease must have the *legal capacity* to enter into a contract and must reach a *meeting of the minds*. The objectives of the lease must be *legal* in nature. The document must be *dated* and must provide for *valid consideration*. The agreed-on terms must be delivered and accepted by both parties.

Statute of Frauds

The primary purpose of the **statute of frauds** is to prevent fraud or disputes over oral agreements. Written, oral, and implied leases are all covered by the statute of frauds in the state in which the property is located. Generally, the statutes require that certain contracts be in writing in order to be enforceable. Although an oral lease agreement of less than one year is usually enforceable if the facts of the situation can be established to the satisfaction of the court, it is wise for the property manager to protect the interests of the owner by executing all leases in writing.

Name of Parties

The lease must contain the names of both the lessor and the lessee and must be signed by the property owner or a legal representative of the owner. All parties should receive a copy of the agreed-on terms.

Liability Alert!

Get Leases Signed

Some landlord-tenant laws permit an enforceable, unsigned lease in some circumstances, so the manager must check local laws. Practically speaking, the manager should make sure that the tenant does not take possession of the premises until after the lease is signed. The requirement for additional signatures from witnesses and an acknowledgment seal from a notary public varies from state to state, but witnesses and notaries generally are not required for leases of less than one year.

Description of the Premises

If the rental property includes land, as when leasing industrial or commercial space, the lease agreement should include a legal description of the property. A lease for an office or apartment must accurately describe the bounds of the space itself. The apartment number and the street address of the building are usually sufficient identification in an apartment lease. For commercial space, a floor plan showing the area to be lease should be appended to the lease. The lease should include a statement of the tenant's right to use common elements, and an itemized list of any furnishings or personal property and their condition should also be attached to the lease.

Term of the Lease

The lease should specify the beginning and termination dates, as well as a statement of the total period it covers. Many leases contain an option to renew: a clause that gives the tenant the right to extend the lease for an additional period of time on specified terms merely by giving sufficient notice of intent. Because options to renew favor the tenant, an owner often will insist on higher rental rates if the option is exercised. Some leases also include a clause allowing tenants to cancel the agreement before the expiration of the term if they pay a penalty.

Possession of the Premises

Property owners in most states are obligated by contract to give the tenant actual occupancy of the premises described in the lease. If the premises are still occupied by a holdover tenant on the date of the new lease, the property owner or an agent of the owner must take action to recover possession and bear the cost of this action. In other states, owners need only convey to the tenant the right of possession. In this case, it is the tenant's obligation to bring any court action necessary to secure actual possession.

Valuable Consideration

All lease contracts must be supported by some type of valid and valuable consideration. Typically, consideration consists of the exchange of promises: the owner promises possession and the tenant promises to pay rent. Whether the lease is gross, net, or percentage, the amount and time of payment must be clearly specified as must the amount of property.

Liability Alert!

Anticipate Changing Circumstances

The longer the lease, the more likely that operating costs, such as taxes and utility costs, will increase over the long haul. The manager should anticipate these possibilities and allow for adjustment of the rental rate when drafting a long-term lease. Most courts will not enforce an increase or reduction in the original amount of rent unless such changes were agreed to in the original contract.

Rental Rate Adjustments

Rental rates may be increased by several methods.

Step-up clause. The **step-up clause** is found in both gross and net leases. Leases with step-up clauses are called *graduated* or *escalation leases*. They provide for specific increases at specific times.

Index lease. Because the income from professional offices, service firms, financial institutions, brokerage houses, and similar businesses cannot be reasonably and effectively adapted to the percentage lease pattern of rental payments, an increase or decrease in their rent is often tied to a selected index of economic conditions. For this reason, such leases are called **index leases.**

The index used in establishing the escalation clause must be reliable and published on a regular and continuing basis by an independent, reputable agency. It should bear a close relationship to the nature of the tenant's business. The most frequently used indexes are the consumer price index (cost-of-living index) and the wholesale price index. The frequency and amount of the adjustments are matters for negotiation between the parties to the lease agreement.

Escalation clause.   An **escalation clause** can be tied to outside factors other than economic indexes, such as union pay scales, taxes, utility rates, and overall operating costs for the premises. When all operating expenses of a building are totaled and charged on a pro rata basis to all tenants, the computation is called a *passthrough.*

Use of the Premises

The property owner may restrict the use of the leased premises by including a special provision in the agreement. For example, restrictive clauses prevalent in office leases might restrict the tenant to using the premises "for the purpose as a general insurance agency only, and for no other purpose." Residential leases will state that the property is to be used for residential purposes only, not for a business (such as opening a child care center) or for an illegal purpose (such as dealing drugs).

Liability Alert!

Restrictive Clauses Must Be Legal

The wording of restrictive clauses must be clear and unambiguous, for the courts will resolve any doubt as to the meaning of a restrictive clause in favor of the party who is restricted by it. In the absence of written restrictions, the tenant may use the premises for any lawful purpose.

Liability Alert!

Watch Out for These "Use of Premises" Pitfalls

Although a residential lease may limit the number of persons who may live in a unit, the manager should be careful when limiting the number of children who can reside in the apartment. While a manager may not refuse to rent just because of familial status, the manager may limit the number of anyone, even children, for safety and sanitation reasons.

Because of the growing number of properties that are being seized for illegal drug activities, it is wise to include a clause in the lease that states that any illegal drug activity is grounds for immediate termination of the tenancy.

Rights and Obligations

The landlord is obligated to provide the property and usually reserves the right to re-enter and to collect rents. Tenants can expect quiet enjoyment of the rental unit and are obligated to pay rent, to not damage the property, and to respect the rights of other tenants.

Building rules.   Most leases for multiple-occupancy buildings include a reference to the "building use guidelines" established to protect the condition, reputation, and safety of the property and to promote compatibility among the occupants. The rules must apply equally to all tenants of the same type.

Assignment and subletting provisions.   Provided that the terms of the lease do not prohibit it, a tenant has the right to assign or sublet his or her interest in the property. **Assignment** of a lease transfers all of the tenant's remaining right in the property to a third party. **Subletting** transfers only part of the interest. Most leases permit the tenant to assign or sublet the rented space only with the owner's prior written approval.

Fire and casualty damage.   Landlords can only insure their buildings and cannot insure the tenant's property. Tenants must acquire their own renters' insurance. State statutes and lease provisions for fire loss, damage, and property restoration vary widely. When drafting a lease, the manager should bear in mind the types and amounts of insurance to be carried on the property, who will pay the premium, and who will receive the proceeds if there is a loss.

Liability Alert!

Comply with the Americans with Disabilities Act (ADA)

All leases should include a compliance clause that identifies which party is responsible for complying with any new local, state, or federal regulations. All leases should now contain language that allocates compliance with the Americans with Disabilities Act (ADA) between the parties. In a few circumstances, if the modifications are too costly or extremely difficult to make, an exemption may be granted. However, no one should assume that an exemption will be granted.

Tenants' Obligations

Tenants are required by law to comply with local building and housing code provisions regarding health and safety. The lease should be clear that tenants are responsible to take good care of the rented space, repair any damage they directly or indirectly cause, and comply with all applicable rules and laws. Tenants are expected to use all plumbing fixtures, elevators, and other facilities in a reasonable manner and should be prohibited in the lease from willfully destroying or damaging the premises, or allowing others to do so, and from disturbing the quiet enjoyment of other tenants.

Tenant improvements.   Tenants should not be allowed to make alterations without advance written consent from the owner, who must be informed of such alterations and protected from all liabilities arising from them. Most tenant improvements to property are classified as fixtures and become part of the real estate. However, a commercial or industrial tenant may be given the right to install *trade* or *chattel fixtures* for business use. These are the personal property of the tenant and may be removed before or on expiration of the lease agreement, provided that the building is restored to its condition when the tenant took possession.

Liability Alert!

Pay Attention to Wording

The wording of the clause that allows the tenant to remove trade fixtures is critical. There is a difference between restoring the property to the condition as of "the tenant's taking of possession," whereas others required restoration only to the condition that prevailed "as of the beginning of the lease." The difference in phraseology can have a major impact on the owner.

Abandoned property. It is in the owner's best interest to include a clause that obligates the tenant to remove personal property from the premises and to clean the rented area at the termination of the lease. Any property left behind is considered abandoned and may be removed from the premises at the tenant's expense. The procedure for handling abandoned personal property in residential and commercial tenancies is often governed by specific state statutes.

Security deposit. State laws vary regarding security deposits, particularly how they can be retained, what documentation is required, and the return within a certain period of time. A **security deposit** may be cash, negotiable securities, or a surety bond. While security deposits are not required by law, some states have imposed a maximum amount allowed for residential security deposits.

Liability Alert!

Know the State Law

Prompted by the Uniform Residential Landlord and Tenant Act, many states have passed security deposit statutes regarding residential security deposits. The laws are detailed and stringent, and the property manager must be aware of his or her state law to develop an equitable and legal policy. If the owner or manager retains any or all of the security deposit, he or she must document the reasons for retention, generally for unpaid rent and/or damages.

Property Owner's Obligations

The landlord/manager also has certain obligations. Unless a net lease is involved, the owner generally is responsible for maintaining the property and to provide certain services, such as snowplowing, grounds keeping, and cleaning certain public areas.

Disclosure and billing. On or before the beginning of a tenancy, the owner should disclose in writing the name and address of the property manager and of the person authorized to receive legal notice on behalf of the owner.

Quiet enjoyment. The owner or property manager grants the tenant a covenant for quiet enjoyment as one of the major benefits in the lease. This right implies a right to possession. Because the tenant is thus given the exclusive use and possession of the space, the terms of the lease must limit the cases in which the owner or manager is allowed on the premises. Most leases allow the manager to enter at any time during an emergency.

Maintaining the premises.   The owner is under no obligation to make repairs unless required to by the lease or statute. Nonetheless, most residential and commercial leases, and even some industrial leases, make the owner responsible for all repairs necessary to keep the premises fit for use. The lease should outline the owner's and tenant's responsibilities for providing services and maintaining the property. The manager should try to draft a lease that relieves the owner of responsibility for maintaining the premises and supply service if compliance is prevented by conditions beyond his or her control. The lease should further state that if the property is sold, the obligations of the owner cease as of the date of sale, with the exception of the responsibility to return or transfer security deposits to the new owner.

Tenant's Remedies for Noncompliance

Tenants have rights when the landlord/agent cannot or does not fulfill the lease obligations.

Noncompliance with rental agreement.   If the property owner or manager fails to perform the required duties, the tenant may sue for damages or terminate the lease by giving the owner the specified notice for breach of contract. If corrective action is not taken within the specified time, the tenant can sue for damages, obtain a court injunction directing the owner to remedy the breach, or terminate the tenancy. If the owner's noncompliance is willful, the tenant may also recover reasonable attorney's fees. Again, the specific rights and enforcement procedures in any situation are determined by state law.

Failure to deliver premises.   Some states require the owner to convey only the right of possession of the leased premises to the tenant. In others, the owner must grant actual occupancy. If the right to possession or actual possession is not conveyed, the tenant does not have to pay rent. The tenant can terminate the rental agreement or sue for specific performance to obtain possession, reasonable damages, and attorney's fees.

Failure to supply essential services. Constructive eviction occurs when the tenant must actually abandon the premises due to the owner's negligence in supplying essential services, such as failing to supply heat or water. Constructive eviction is recognized by most state courts as the basis for terminating the lease, for an action to recover possession, or for a suit for damages.

Partial eviction occurs when a tenant is unable to use part or all of the premises for the purposes intended in the lease due to some failure by the owner. In cases of partial eviction, state statutes sometimes allow the tenant to take appropriate measures to obtain the services needed and then deduct the cost from the rental payments. In other cases, the tenant may simply be allowed to withhold rent until the breach of contract is corrected.

Liability Alert!

Protect Against Constructive and Partial Eviction

For the owner's protection, the lease should require the tenant to give notice of any failure and allow the owner time to remedy the situation before the tenant claims constructive eviction. Some state statutes prohibit the cutoff of utilities to residential tenants, even if rent or utility payments are owed to the owner.

Owner's Remedies for Noncompliance

Tenants can lose their lease if they do not comply with the rental agreement. Examples include not paying rent on time or not at all, seriously damaging the property, bothering other tenants with excessive sound, and so on.

Noncompliance with rental agreement. The owner is provided with certain remedies in case the tenant fails to meet the terms of the lease. According to most leases, the owner may deliver written notice to the tenant stating the nature of any contract breach and calling for the tenant to repair the breach within a reasonable time to prevent termination of the lease.

The lease should further state that if the tenant fails to repair or replace damaged items, the owner or owner's agent may enter the premises and have the necessary work performed. An itemized bill for the reasonable cost of the work may be presented to the tenant, due with the next rental payment. The lease also should provide that if the owner chooses to terminate the lease, the bill comes due immediately on presentation.

Suit for eviction. Eviction proceedings can be brought against a tenant for several reasons: nonpayment of rent, illegal possession of the premises after termination of the lease, unlawful use of the premises, nonpayment of charges attributed to the tenant under the terms of the lease, and certain other breaches of the lease contract. When a tenant has failed to perform in one of these areas, the owner may file a court suit for recovery of the premises after giving the tenant legal notice.

This proceeding is commonly known as a *suit for eviction*, a *suit for possession*, or a *forcible entry and detainer suit*. If the court issues a judgment decree for possession in favor of the owner, the tenant must peaceably leave or the owner can have the decree enforced by an officer of the court, who will then forcibly remove the tenant and the tenant's belongings. This process is known as *actual eviction*.

Default. Because statutes regarding a tenant's default under the terms of a lease vary from state to state, the lease should include a clause to the effect that if the tenant defaults on rent payments, the owner or manager can terminate the tenancy.

Bankruptcy. Because of changing federal bankruptcy laws and court decisions interpreting them, property managers should review bankruptcy default clauses in leases with an attorney.

Illegal activities. Language in the lease should be very clear prohibiting certain activities, such as drug trafficking, felony crimes, or threatening other tenants or the manager.

Lease Formats

Standard lease forms are usually available through the Internet and local real estate and professional management organizations. These may be combined with riders and addenda to cover almost any leasing situation. Many larger management firms and property owners have developed standard leases that may be modified to cover most eventualities. Larger buildings, particularly commercial ones, may also utilize their own lease forms. One of the advantages of using a standard form is that the property manager can become thoroughly familiar with its provisions and legal ramifications. On the other hand, standard leases often require revision and may be out of date.

Liability Alert!

Don't Practice Law without a License

Unless the property manager is a lawyer, he or she should not write lease clauses or any form of legal statement that may bind the owner. The manager's or the owner's attorney should advise the parties about leases and riders.

■ Managing Tenant Relations

Landlords' and tenants' interests are not mutually exclusive, and the two do not need to be in constant conflict. The ultimate success of a property manager will largely depend on his or her ability to maintain good relations with tenants. Dissatisfied tenants eventually vacate the property, and a high tenant turnover means greater expense for the owner. If a manager is ineffective for long, the owner's profits will disappear as tenants move out, expenses increase, and unpaid past-due notices pile up. A good manager is tactful and decisive and will act to the benefit of both owner and occupants.

Move-In Inspections

At the beginning of the tenancy, the manager should inspect the premises with the tenant to determine if promised repairs or alterations have been made or are in progress. Both the manager and the tenant should sign the form, each should keep a copy, and the same form should be used at the time the tenant leaves. Putting it in writing helps avoid potential disagreements at the end of the lease.

> ## Liability Alert!
>
> ### Avoid Costly Misunderstandings
>
> Misunderstandings can be avoided by a letter from the manager outlining the procedures tenants should follow when moving out. When a security deposit is refunded to a tenant, it should be accompanied by another letter explaining any deductions from the deposit. (In fact, this is usually required by law.)

Clear Understanding of Lease Terms

At the outset of each tenancy, the manager should establish a basic understanding with the tenant on all matters relating to the lease terms. A tenant brochure that outlines all policies and procedures should be given to each new tenant. The tenant should be told of the penalties for failure to comply with building regulations.

Handling Maintenance Requests

Maintenance is the single most important factor over which the property manager has control. The manager should insist that all maintenance requests be submitted in writing. Then, a system should be developed to quickly and effectively channel service requests to the appropriate parties. One way is to use carbonless paper forms of three different colors, one each for the manager, the service person, and the tenant. (See Figure 4.1.)

The success of tenant relations also depends to a great extent on the speed of the landlord's response to the tenant's needs. Whenever a service request is made, the tenant should be told immediately when it will be taken care of, or told that it will not be done.

Rent Collections

For convenience, accuracy, and speed in rent collection and record keeping, most monthly rentals are due and payable on the first of the month. From the outset, the manager should be clear as to when rent is due, where it is to be paid, and the penalties for being late or not making the payment. The manager should follow an established procedure that is rigidly adhered to without exception. Tenants should never be accommodated at the expense of the owner.

Lease Renewals

Unless the lease agreement includes an automatic renewal clause, it will expire on the date specified in the contract. A stable tenant with a record of timely rental payments is a proven quantity and an asset to the owner. Further, the present tenant will probably make fewer demands for redecorating or other alterations than a new occupant would, representing additional savings.

Rent Increases

On the surface, both the tenant and the manager dislike rental increases. The tenant does not want to pay more; the manager fears a high vacancy rate will discredit his or her professional reputation. However, the tenant and the manager must accept the economic realities involved in making real estate investments show a profit. It is advisable to explain, if possible, the reason for the higher rates, which could possibly include upgrades, major repairs, more amenities, and more service.

Figure 4.1 | Maintenance Request Form

LINCOLN PROPERTY COMPANY
Maintenance Request

No. 34456

	DEAD BOLT INFO.	RECEIVED	COMPLETED

APT. #

NAME

TELEPHONE NO.   UNABLE TO
                         ENTER

WORK REQUESTED: PARTS TO BE
                                         ORDERED:

                                         DATE ORDERED:

                                         DELIVERY SCHEDULED:

                                         REMARKS:

UNABLE TO COMPLETE BECAUSE:

                                 SPECIAL LOCK   APARTMENT CONDITION

                                 PET   GOOD   POOR

                                 FILTER CHANGE
ASSIGNED TO   COMPLETED BY   TAKEN BY

ORIGINAL

Source: Courtesy of Property Company of America. Used with permission.

Notice of the new rates should be given to the tenants more than 30 days before the lease renewal and possibly as much as three to six months in advance.

Terminating the Tenancy

Notice of intent to vacate must be given within a certain period, which should be specified in the terms of the lease agreement. A letter prior to move-out can include a checklist for the tenant, detailing the expected cleaning, postoccupancy inspections, return of security deposit, and so on.

Terminating the Tenancy in Court

Eviction suit. If possible, before legal action can be taken, the tenant must always be given notice of the breach or improper conduct and an opportunity to rectify the situation. During a grace period of three to five days, the tenant should be sent a reminder notice that states the penalty and a warning of further action to be taken if payment is not received immediately.

> ### Liability Alert!
> #### Know State Statutes Regarding Eviction
> The manager should be aware of not only state statutes but also the local rules that may apply. State statutes dictate the minimum number of days before suit can be filed, what notice must be given, and the forms that must be filed.

Actual removal. Once the court gives a judgment returning possession to the landlord, or the landlord is successful at a trial, the property manager must determine whether the tenant has physically left the premises. If the tenant refuses to vacate the property even after the court rules for the landlord, the landlord must secure a court order and the sheriff or constable serving the court will physically remove the tenant from the property.

case study

Jennifer Chin manages a 75-unit apartment complex. In one week, she was faced with three tenant "situations."

1. For the last three months, tenant Thompson paid the rent only after receiving the landlord's eviction notice. This month, Thompson is late again.
2. Tenant Samuels has made repeated requests for various services and repairs, most of which have not been the landlord's responsibility. When Chin told him tactfully that the landlord was not obligated to repaint in the middle of a one-year tenancy, he threatened a "tenant revolt."
3. Tenant Juarez, a model tenant for five years, told Chin that she would not be renewing her lease when it expired in two months. Juarez said she was "uncomfortable with building policies."

Case Study Review

1. Based on Chin's experience with Thompson, who consistently pays late, what can Chin to do prevent late payments in the future?
   a. Hire an attorney on a monthly basis to handle legal evictions
   b. Put a notice in her "to do" file to notify Thompson a week before rent is due
   c. Revise her leases to include a provision for a late penalty to encourage on-time payments
   d. Accept the fact that some tenants are just late payers

2. The issues with tenants Samuel and Juarez indicate
- **a.** lax management style from Chin.
- **b.** Chin has a good relationship with the tenants.
- **c.** possible problems with Chin's management style.
- **d.** reasons for Chin to start looking for another job.

■ Summary

A landlord leases property to tenants granting tenants the right to occupy the premises for a specified period of time in exchange for some form of compensation and subject to certain responsibilities and restrictions. The tenant's right to occupy the property during the term of the lease agreement is called a leasehold estate, or interest, in the property. There are four kinds of leasehold estates: estate for years, estate from period to period, tenancy at will, and tenancy at sufferance.

The requirements for a valid lease are similar to those for any legally binding contract: parties legal to contract, description of the property, specific term, valid consideration, and for a legal purpose. All parties should receive a signed copy of the agreed-on terms (delivered and accepted). Leases for more than a year must be in writing to be enforceable under the statute of frauds.

The method by which the tenant pays rent determines the type of lease contract. The three basic forms are the gross lease, usually used with residential space; the net lease, common to office and industrial space; and the percentage lease, for most retail space.

Commonly, leases include rules for occupancy and restriction on the use of the premises. Building rules and regulations can be a separate attachment and should be reviewed by both parties to prevent misunderstandings.

A management firm can develop its own standard lease form that can be modified to cover most leasing situations, or it may obtain them through the Internet or local real estate organizations. Because any standard lease will probably have to be tailored to fit each specific situation, legal counsel should always be consulted.

The manager must protect the owner's interests by setting up an effective system for collecting rent and coping with uncooperative tenants. When service requests are made, the tenant should be told immediately either when the job will be done or why it cannot be completed. Under most lease agreements, tenants must give notice of intent to terminate within a specific period. The owner has the right to bring a court suit for eviction and a judgment for damages against any delinquent or disruptive tenant. Security deposits must be administered according to state law.

■ Review Questions

True-False

1. Whatever their differences in types of properties managed or other general or specific duties, all property managers have responsibility for leasing the premises.
   a. True
   b. False

2. The leasehold estate most commonly used by property managers in renting residential, commercial, and industrial space is the estate at will.
   a. True
   b. False

3. When a tenant remains in possession of the property after the expiration of the lease term, with or without the owner's consent, he or she is referred to as a "holdover tenant."
   a. True
   b. False

4. If a tenant retains possession of the property without the owner's consent, the situation is called a "tenancy at sufferance."
   a. True
   b. False

5. Under a gross lease, the tenant pays a fixed rental amount, and the owner pays all other expenses.
   a. True
   b. False

6. A percentage lease is used primarily in industrial properties.
   a. True
   b. False

7. Written, oral, and implied leases are all covered by a state's statute of frauds.
   a. True
   b. False

8. Contract is to consideration as lease is to rent.
   a. True
   b. False

9. Subletting transfers all of a tenant's remaining rights in the property to a third party.
   a. True
   b. False

10. The ADA requires that owners of commercial properties remodel or modify their units to achieve accessibility, regardless of the cost.
    a. True
    b. False

Multiple-Choice

1. Which creates good tenant relations?
   a. Inconsistent maintenance of the property
   b. Little communication with the tenants
   c. Lax enforcement of the building rules
   d. Clear understanding of the rules and regulations

2. Of the following, the best tool for good landlord-tenant relations is
   a. many rules.
   b. move-in inspections.
   c. vague understanding of lease terms.
   d. varying rental rates from the same units.

3. How should the manager deal with maintenance requests?
   a. Ignore them unless repeated three times
   b. Process once a week, preferably on Monday mornings
   c. Tell the tenant when the repair will be made or why it won't be done
   d. Procrastinate and evade the issue

4. What is the benefit of a stable, satisfied tenant population?
   a. Threatens earning capabilities of the building
   b. Improves stability of property income
   c. Increases manager's time showing units
   d. Increases renovation costs

5. How can the manager encourage prompt rental payments?
   a. Accept valid excuses for late payments if made before the due date
   b. Begin with clear-cut understanding as to when and where payments are due
   c. Avoid charging late fees
   d. Shun offering incentives for early payments

6. All of the following would be bargaining factors when it comes time to renew the lease *EXCEPT* the
   a. discussion of the national origin of other tenants.
   b. length of new lease term.
   c. extent of redecorating.
   d. rental amount increase.

7. How can a manager avoid tenant protest over a rent increase?
   a. Short notice, less than 30 days
   b. No explanation for the rent increase
   c. Decrease services
   d. Long notice, three to six months in advance

8. The tenant has to leave the premises when the landlord fails to provide essential services. This is an example of
   a. actual eviction.
   b. constructive eviction.
   c. partial eviction.
   d. forced eviction.

9. Tenant relations can be aided by
   a. contacting tenants only on an emergency basis.
   b. saving brochures to distribute only when a problem arises.
   c. reviewing rent collection procedures with the tenant in a conference at the beginning of a lease.
   d. associating with tenants on a social basis.

10. If a landlord intends to keep part or all of a security deposit, he or she
    a. need not give the tenant an itemized statement explaining the withholding of the deposit.
    b. should just keep the money with no other obligation.
    c. may not be able to retain all or part of the deposit because of damages caused by the tenant.
    d. should follow state laws in regard to time periods.

11. If rents are increased, the manager should
    a. schedule a vacation for the day the increase is announced.
    b. expect an organized tenant protest and hire extra security.
    c. learn the logic behind the increase so that he or she can explain it to the tenants.
    d. decrease maintenance service.

12. The time between the rent due and the announcement of action for recovery should be
    a. three days.
    b. five days.
    c. adjusted according to the tenant's circumstances.
    d. a fixed, determined period.

13. On termination by a tenant, the property manager should
    a. contact the tenant immediately to get a referral for a new tenant.
    b. schedule an immediate discontinuance of utilities.
    c. inspect the space after the tenant has removed all personal property.
    d. make sure the tenant does not discuss plans for leaving with other tenants.

14. What form should the manager use when inspecting the property after the tenant has vacated?

    a. Tenant exit interview form

    b. Original lease

    c. List of concessions previously made

    d. Move-in/move-out checklist

15. In most states, detailed and stringent security deposit statutes have been passed. Which is generally a provision of these statutes?

    a. The landlord need not document any charges against the security deposit.

    b. The landlord must itemize the deductions in a written statement.

    c. Deductions are not authorized for nonstandard decorating, excessive cleaning charges, and damages to the premises.

    d. The tenant may apply the deposit to the last month's rent.

chapter five

Managing Residential Properties

■ Key Terms

blockbusting

cash flow report

Civil Rights Act of 1866

Civil Rights Act of 1968

common elements

condominiums

cooperatives

covenants, conditions, and restrictions (CC&Rs)

disability

duplexes

management pricing worksheet

operating budget

operating costs

proprietary lease

protected classes

reserve funds

resident manager

scattered-site rentals

steering

testers

triplexes

learning objectives

On completing this chapter, you will be able to

■ distinguish among the various types of residential property;

■ recognize the special challenges of managing condominiums and cooperatives;

■ explain how fair housing laws affect property management; and

■ describe how the manager assembles reports to help owners make informed decisions about the property.

■ Residential Housing: The Big Picture

Residential rental housing ranges from single-family houses to huge apartment projects of several thousand units in multiple buildings and includes condominiums, cooperatives, and retirement communities, as well as such special-purpose housing as manufactured home parks, time-sharing resorts, and apartment hotels.

Government-assisted and institutional housing also are included under the broad "residential" umbrella. While specific application of the property management techniques discussed in this chapter may have to be modified to the circumstance, the basic principles here have universal application.

Property managers should research and follow the laws and regulations of the jurisdiction where the property is located. Compliance with fair housing laws is of particular concern in residential management.

■ Types of Residential Property

Different types of dwellings require unique management capabilities. This chapter discusses **scattered-site rentals**—single-family residences, **duplexes, triplexes,** and large apartment communities, in addition to the challenges of managing condominium and cooperative communities.

Single-Family Homes, Duplexes, and Triplexes

Investing in single-family homes has been popular for some time, and many owners have built up large holdings of single-family dwellings. These homes generally are managed by their owners if they live in the city where the homes are located; if not, the owners hire professional managers.

It may be unprofitable or impractical for a professional property manager who manages other types of property to manage one single-family home or a few duplexes or triplexes. The principal difference between managing single-family homes and managing apartments is geography and time because scattered-site rentals are often located in various parts of a city. Properly maintaining and showing properties to prospective tenants may involve unproductive travel to and from various locations.

Even with the most skillful and well-organized management, the financial return on single-family home rental is marginal at best, compared to alternate uses of investment funds. If interest rates on mortgages are high, cash flow may be negative. Further, many owners will agree to a below-market rent in exchange for a tenant who will take care of the property and remain in it for a long period of time.

Duplexes and triplexes with common areas, including front, side, and backyards, require harmonious cooperation among occupants. Thus, the tenants must be compatible, a condition not usually as strong a factor when renting in larger communities.

Multifamily Properties

The term *multifamily properties* is commonly understood to mean apartment buildings of five or more units. Housing alternatives range from fully furnished units, where everything is supplied for the tenant, to unfurnished apartments equipped only with floors and walls, with the standard unit lying somewhere in between.

In any type of residential rental housing, the kind and number of facilities provided will have a direct effect on the property manager's workload; swimming pools, laundry rooms, and parking areas increase the maintenance activities for the premises. These facilities and services affect the overall desirability and influence the rental structure of any type of residential rental complex, commanding more in rents to offset the extra maintenance activities.

Condominium and Cooperative Ownership

As land and construction costs become more expensive, people are turning to less expensive forms of housing, such as cooperatives and condominiums.

From a management perspective, these specialized forms of residential management share many characteristics of ordinary multiple-occupancy structures, but the form of ownership changes the manager's goals and objectives. Additionally, managers do not have the responsibility of maintaining occupancy levels.

Liability Alert!

Be Aware of Special Requirements

Before entering agreements to manage either cooperative or condominium communities, the manager should closely study local and state laws and governing documents. Legal structures are complex and vary even within the same state. More states are requiring a property manager license, community association manager license, or real estate license. The trend toward increasing regulation and licensing requirements is likely to continue with other states.

The advantage of managing cooperatives (and condominiums) over apartment buildings is that members occupying their own units generally take more pride in their surroundings. However, they also want to be more informed about management policies and practices. The property manager should try to avoid pitfalls of the possible fractious differences of opinion by acting only with the full approval of the board of directors and by being responsible only to the board. The property manager must be familiar with corporate law and procedure and have an experienced attorney available for consultation.

Cooperatives. In cooperative ownership, the apartment owner purchases shares in the corporation (or partnership or trust) that holds title to the entire apartment building. The ownership of the building can be either trust or corporate in nature. The principal asset of the cooperative is the building. The co-op shareholder receives a **proprietary lease** granting occupancy of a specific unit in the building. The cooperative owns the building, and the shareholder owns a lease (personal property).

The owner occupies the unit under the terms of the lease but does not own it. Each lessee must pay a pro rata share of the corporation's expenses, which include any mortgage charges, real estate taxes, maintenance, payroll, and such. The owner can deduct a proportionate share of the taxes and interest charges for tax purposes (provided 80 percent of a cooperative's income is derived from tenant-owner rentals).

In a cooperative, the property manager's first responsibility is to fulfill corporate aims on behalf of the shareholders. This usually includes maintaining the property's physical integrity, ensuring services to the occupants, and submitting regular operating reports to the board of directors. The precise services rendered can range from a periodic consultation to full-time management services on a fixed-fee basis.

The aims of the corporation and the services expected from the manager should always be spelled out in a detailed written contract.

Liability Alert!

Be Alert for Possible Discriminatory Practices

All prospective purchases of proprietary leases generally must be approved by the board of directors. Sometimes, this process has been used for discriminatory purposes. A property manager considering employment by a cooperative should avoid associating with any group he or she suspects of discrimination.

Condominiums.   Condominium ownership estates in real property consist of an individual interest in an apartment or commercial unit and an undivided common interest in the common areas in the condo project, such as the land, parking areas, elevators, stairways, and exterior structure. Each condominium unit is a statutory entity that may be mortgaged, taxed, sold, or otherwise transferred in ownership independently of all other units in the condo project. Units are separately assessed and taxed. Condos are governed by an elected association and board of directors.

The rapid expansion of the residential condominium market has opened new opportunities for property managers. Condominium management is concerned mainly with maintaining the integrity of the premises, ensuring ongoing service to occupants, and attaining other mutual goals of the owners. Before taking over an association, the manager should thoroughly read the **covenants, conditions, and restrictions (CC&Rs),** carefully study recent operating reports, and review the amounts in any reserve funds.

The manager is usually responsible for billing and collecting assessments and keeping accounting records for the homeowners' association. Generally, the manager maintains all common areas and provides the cost data necessary to draw up an operating budget and make individual assessments for maintenance and reserves, constantly balancing the owners' desires for lower maintenance fees against the need to spend money to preserve the property. Thus, the typical method of determining management fees based on a percentage of money collected may be inappropriate, since the more the manager increases fees, the more the manager earns.

Liability Alert!

Protect Your Interests

Because the condo owners' association governing board is an elected body that changes frequently, the manager should negotiate a contract for a guaranteed and reasonably long term. Otherwise, the manager may never receive adequate compensation for the time and effort expended in managing the property. The management contract should specify the amount of compensation and other terms of the agreement (hours, cancellation, etc.).

■ Tenant Relations and Fair Housing Laws

Federal fair housing laws (as well as state and city fair housing laws) are designed to guarantee everyone an equal opportunity to live wherever they can afford and choose to live. Fair housing laws will not eliminate discrimination, but they do prevent a property manager or owner from arbitrarily rejecting a rental application based on race, color, religion, national origin, sex, familial status, disability, or other legally protected characteristics.

Civil Rights Act of 1866

Under the **Civil Rights Act of 1866,** "all citizens shall have the same rights as white citizens to inherit, purchase, lease, sell, hold and convey real and personal property." There are no exceptions to this prohibition against discrimination based on race. The Civil Rights Act of 1866 was held constitutional by the Supreme Court in the case of *Jones v. Alfred H. Mayer Company* in June 1968, shortly after the **Civil Rights Act of 1968** was passed, which permitted racial discrimination in certain instances.

According to the court, The Civil Rights Act of 1866 *"prohibits all racial discrimination*, private or public, in the sale or rental of real property" (emphasis added). Under no circumstances is it legal to turn people down simply because of race or color.

Fair Housing Act (Title VIII of the Civil Rights Act of 1968)

The federal Fair Housing Act passed in 1968 originally only prohibited discrimination based on race, color, religion, and national origin. In 1974, sex was added as a protected class, and in 1988, two more **protected classes**—familial status and disability—were added. States and cities may not remove any of the protected classes, but they can add other protected classes. Originally, the term *minorities* was used, but today, as a reflection of what minorities really mean, they are referred to as protected classes.

A property manager or owner may not, for discriminatory reasons, do any of the following:

- Refuse to show, rent, or negotiate with a person for housing
- Discriminate in the terms of conditions of a lease
- Engage in discriminatory advertising
- Tell potential renters that a property is not available, if in fact it is
- Interfere with, coerce, threaten, or intimidate a person to keep him or her from taking advantage of the full benefits of the federal Fair Housing Act
- Engage in blockbusting or steering

Discriminatory advertising.   Inappropriate advertising includes using references to race, color, religion, sex, national origin, familial status, or disability in any advertising. Property managers should avoid using terms that imply integrated or segregated neighborhoods or buildings. It is also unlawful to use human models in advertising to indicate exclusiveness based on race, color, religion, sex, handicap, familial status, or national origin. When human models are used in advertising, the models should reasonably represent the majority and minority groups in the community, both sexes, and families with children.

Blockbusting.   Blockbusting is the act of encouraging people to sell or rent by claiming that the entry of a protected class into the area will have some negative impact on property values. It is illegal to assert that the presence of certain persons (i.e., protected classes) will cause property values to decline, that crime and antisocial behavior will increase, or that the quality of schools will decline.

A message from the manager or rental agent that the property or neighborhood is "undergoing changes" because a "certain group" is moving in may be viewed as *blockbusting*. Another term for this activity is *panic selling.*

Steering.   Property managers should be especially careful to avoid **steering,** which is the channeling of members of protected classes to buildings or neighborhoods that are already occupied primarily by members of those same classes and away from buildings and neighborhoods occupied primarily by members of other classes. Steering can be very subtle and difficult to detect, and it can also be unintentional when the manager is not even aware of his or her own discriminatory assumptions.

Historically, managers were steering when they put white tenants in one building or on one floor and all of the Asian Americans, African Americans, or any nonwhites in another building or floor. A more current example of steering is congregating all families with children in one building or on one floor away from tenants without children.

Steering may also occur when the manager tells the prospect that there is no vacancy, when, in fact, there is a vacancy. This misstatement, which is illegal when it is made on the basis of any of the protected classes, steers the prospect away from the manager's building.

Equal housing poster.   Failure to post the equal housing opportunity poster may be considered *prima facie* evidence of discrimination. The poster can be obtained form the U.S. Department of Housing and Urban Development. (See Figure 5.1.)

The equal housing logo should also be used in all display advertising and printed materials. The logo does not have to be included in classified ads, so long as the newspaper prints a fair housing nondiscrimination disclaimer at the beginning of the rental section, as shown in Figure 5.2.

Familial status.   The minimum for establishing familial status is the presence of at least one individual in the family who is under the age of 18, or the presence of a pregnant woman, or one who has or is obtaining custody of children. Landlords, condominiums, and cooperatives may not exclude children from living in their communities, unless the community meets specific HUD requirements to qualify as elderly or near elderly.

Communities and managers may not arbitrarily decide to avoid children. There are only three situations in which housing providers may refuse to rent to a family with children:

1. Housing that is provided by a state or federal program designed to assist older persons
2. Housing that is intended for and solely occupied by those 62 years or older

Figure 5.1 | Equal Housing Opportunity Poster

U.S. Department of Housing and Urban Development

EQUAL HOUSING
OPPORTUNITY

We Do Business in Accordance With the Federal Fair Housing Law

(The Fair Housing Amendments Act of 1988)

It is Illegal to Discriminate Against Any Person Because of Race, Color, Religion, Sex, Handicap, Familial Status, or National Origin

- In the sale or rental of housing or residential lots
- In advertising the sale or rental of housing
- In the financing of housing

- In the provision of real estate brokerage services
- In the appraisal of housing
- Blockbusting is also illegal

Anyone who feels he or she has been discriminated against may file a complaint of housing discrimination:
1-800-669-9777 (Toll Free)
1-800-927-9275 (TDD)

U.S. Department of Housing and
Urban Development
Assistant Secretary for Fair Housing and
Equal Opportunity
Washington, D.C. 20410

Previous editions are obsolete   form HUD-928.1A (2/2003)

3. Housing designed for older persons in which at least 80 percent of the housing is occupied by at least one person who is aged 55 or older

Disability. The protected class based on disability includes both the physically and mentally disabled. A **disability** is defined as a physical or mental impairment that substantially limits one or more of a person's major life activities. For example, those who cannot see, hear, walk, speak, or learn would be considered disabled. Also protected are those with HIV or AIDS. Note that disabilities caused by current illegal drug use are not covered.

Generally, landlords are not required to modify their units built before March 13, 1991, to fit the special needs of the disabled, although they must let their disabled

Figure 5.2 | Equal Housing Opportunity Classified Ads

EQUAL HOUSING
OPPORTUNITY

All real estate advertised in this newspaper is subject to the federal and state Fair Housing Act which makes it illegal to advertise "any preference, limitation or discrimination based on race, color, religion, sex, handicap, familial status or national origin, or an intention to make any such preference, limitation, or discrimination."

The newspaper will not knowingly accept any advertising for real estate which is in violation of the law. All persons are hereby informed that all dwellings advertised are available on an equal opportunity basis.

tenants make any necessary modifications. (These tenants may be required to return the premises to its original condition at the end of the lease term.) Guide dogs and "fetch" dogs utilized by those in wheelchairs may not be considered pets as a method of keeping the blind or wheelchair-bound tenant out of the property.

Liability Alert!

Differences between ADA and Fair Housing Requirements

Any newly constructed multifamily building (with five or more units) that was ready for occupancy after March 1991 must allow access and use by disabled persons (e.g., by including wheelchair ramps and elevators). It is not sufficient to "build to the local code." The federal guidelines mandate design minimums that must be followed, even if the local codes differ. Not all architects are aware of the requirements, and building to ADA code does not always satisfy accessibility requirements for private dwellings covered by the federal Fair Housing Act.

Multifamily property and asset managers should consult the *HUD Design Manual* available through HUD's Fair Housing Information Clearinghouse at 800-343-3442. Enforcement may include financial penalties as well as remedial action on a nonconforming property.

Testers. Discriminatory practices are often difficult to prove, so **testers** are often used to gather evidence for fair housing complaints. Two or more testers might represent themselves to landlords as prospective tenants and then take note of any differences in treatment. Anyone may be a tester, not just a person who has been specially trained. As a matter of practice, managers should treat everyone equally, without exception, without regard to race, color, religion, national origin, sex, familial status, or disability.

Enforcement. A complaint may be filed directly with HUD, or, more commonly, with a local city or state human rights agency. If conciliation is unsuccessful, either the case will be heard by an *Administrative Law Judge (ALJ)* or brought as a civil action in the appropriate U.S. district or state court. The burden of proof falls on the complainant who must prove that the discrimination occurred.

When cases end up in court, fines may be levied: up to $11,000 for the first offense; up to $27,500 for the second offense in five years; and up to $55,000 for more than two offenses in a seven-year period. The time limitation pertains to real estate companies. There are no time limitations for multiple offenses by individuals. The fines are paid to the United States, not to the aggrieved person.

An aggrieved person can obtain an award of *actual damages* and injunctive relief in either administrative or federal court. In a court action, however, a judge or jury can award unlimited *punitive damages* to the aggrieved party. Also, the prevailing party may be awarded reasonable attorney's fees and costs.

Liability Alert!

Avoiding Fair Housing Violations

To avoid any allegations of illegal discrimination, the property manager should do all of the following:

- Prominently display the equal housing poster

- Develop a written fair housing policy that affirms management's commitment to equal housing opportunity

- Provide fair housing training for all employees

- Designate someone in the office to be the "fair housing officer," to be responsible for keeping current and answering employee questions

- Discuss fair housing objectives and requirements on regular basis at staff meetings

- Make sure that tenant selection is objective, relevant to fulfilling lease obligations, and applied equally to every applicant

- Keep detailed, comprehensive records of each prospect and inquiry

---

■ Residential Market Analysis

Market surveys of comparable residential properties and economic conditions in the immediate area are absolutely essential in gauging any property's viability as an income-producing investment and in establishing a rental schedule for the apartments.

Establishing a Rental Schedule

Many managers will shop other properties to see the space that is being rented by competitors and the amenities being offered, and to determine their value. Reading the competitor's advertising is another way to learn of competing market values.

Gauging Profitability

It is not sufficient for the manager merely to be aware of the total number of persons in an area; he or she must also know the size of the average family to determine the type and number of housing units needed. The manager must also analyze current population shifts in terms of land use and income level. The implications for the future of the neighborhood and for the manager's property are quite different between an increase that stems from an influx of middle-income families into an expanding community and one that is due to overcrowding in low-rent buildings.

■ Maintaining the Apartment Building

The precise duties of all employees involved in maintaining a property depend on the size and facilities of the building, the condition of the premises, and the terms of the management contract. Maintenance duties may be carried out by a large staff that includes a resident manager, janitorial staff, on-site maintenance crew, and various outside service contractors. The resident manager for a smaller property may have to assume maintenance responsibilities with no on-site support whatsoever.

Maintenance Personnel

The manager's decision to hire full-time or contract services must be based on the amount of services required and the cost-effectiveness to the owner. Hiring decisions should be made on the experience and versatility of the applicant.

Resident Manager's Responsibilities

The resident manager is one of the most important people on the management team as this may be the only person the tenant ever meets. Consequently, the **resident manager** must possess a variety of skills: able to manage tenants and maintenance personnel, adept at accounting for money and supplies, and aware of community issues and tenant concerns, all the while balancing the owner's wishes with the tenant's demands.

The resident manager is usually responsible for supervising maintenance, housekeeping, and maintenance of common interior areas. The resident manager should visit the apartment with the new tenant using the "move-in, move-out" checklist previously mentioned. Also, the resident manager is generally expected to "walk" the property at least daily to note any problems that might need to be remedied.

Liability Alert!

Supervising the Resident Manager

Because the property manager is not usually in daily contact with each building, the resident manager should submit weekly reports on the condition of the property, the work performed, and jobs anticipated for the upcoming week. When coupled with monthly inspection tours, these reports reveal a lot about the resident manager's performance and attitude.

■ Apartment Operating Reports

Owners of apartment buildings have the same need for operating reports as owners of commercial and industrial properties. Several reports can provide the owner with the raw data necessary to evaluate the property manager, determine the value of the investment, and decide on the best course of action.

Apartment Operating Budgets

Apartment occupancy rates are always subject to change because of economic conditions, such as employment cuts or the addition of new units to the market. When preparing a budget, a property manager should determine if there are any predictable influences in the market for the coming budget year that might affect occupancy. For example, in periods of high occupancy, it is important to know what new projects are under construction and when they will be available for leasing. Long periods of low vacancy rates in a community usually cause new apartments to be constructed. A study of lease expiration dates in such situations should also be made to analyze the vulnerability of the manager's apartments to losses from move-outs to newer units. Essentially, the **operating budget** tells the owner the net operating income before debt service (mortgage payment). To calculate net operating income, subtract the total expenses from the total annual anticipated income. (See Figure 5.3.)

Additional Income

The manager should be aware of any possible sources of income. In addition to the rents, parking and storage fees and vending and laundry machines can provide additional income. Operating expenses for apartment buildings can be allocated to four major categories: taxes, insurance, maintenance, and administration.

The form in Figure 5.4 is consistent with the National Apartment Association (NAA) and the Institute of Real Estate Management (IREM).

Figure 5.3 | Operating Budget

Operating Budget		
Income		
4 studio @ $550/month	$26,400	
6 one-bedroom @ $650/month	46,800	
7 two-bedroom @ $800/month	67,200	
Gross scheduled rental income	$140,400	
5% vacancy and rent loss	(7,020)	
Gross collectible rental income	$133,380	
Income from other sources	5,500	
Total Anticipated Revenue		$138,880
Expenses		
Real estate taxes	$12,960	
Salaries	22,550	
Utilities	9,990	
Supplies	2,700	
Maintenance and repairs	5,500	
Insurance	3,000	
Administrative	1,875	
Management @ 5% gross income	6,669	
Reserves	7,500	
Total Expenses		$72,744
Net Operating Income before Debt Service		$66,136
Debt Service ($200,000 @ 7% constant)	$14,000	
Cash Flow		$52,136

Figure 5.4 | Cash Flow

Cash Flow Report			
Property: Garden Arms Apartments		**Month: February**	**Year: 2004**
Income			
Gross potential income	$30,000		
less vacancy, rent loss, and delinquencies	2,500		
Effective Gross Income		$27,500	
Other Income			
laundry	200		
vending	200		
parking	200		
storage	300	900	
Gross Operating Income			$28,400
Expenses			
Wages			
property manager	1,500		
resident manager	700		
staff	3,000	5,200	
Variable expenses			
utilities	1,000		
maintenance	800		
professional fees	1,100	2,900	
Fixed expenses			
property tax	650		
insurance	500	1,150	
Total Operating Expenses			$9,250
Net Operating Income			$19,150
Capital expenditures			
rugs	650		
drapes	50		
appliances and fixtures	1,000	1,700	
Debt Service	8,000		
Less Capital Expenditures and Debt Service			$9,700
Cash Flow			$9,450

After-Tax Cash Flow Analysis

Although cash flow projections appear to be complex, they deal only with previously used data to show the effect that the investment property has on the owner's income in terms of tax benefits. The after-tax cash flow analysis allows the owner to analyze actual return on investment after taxes and decide whether it is economically more advantageous to keep the property, invest more money in it, refinance it, or sell it. The owner may also use the manager's operating reports, particularly the cash flow, as a "report card" or measure of the manager's performance by comparing it from period to period.

For example, assume an older apartment building has a reliable gross income of $100,000 per year. Its operating cost rate is 50 percent, including capital expenditures and reserves. At the beginning of the year, its depreciable tax base was $400,000, and $5,000 was spent for capital improvements. Straight-line depreciation is computed based on an economic life of 27½ years. Assume that the owner is in a 28 percent income tax bracket, and the entire amount of capital expenditures is depreciable for one full year.

When calculating taxable income, those capital expenditures for additions or other major repairs that extend the life of the property or markedly increase its value should be added to the basis of the property and depreciated over its life, rather than being currently deducted as an operating cost. The property carries a $300,000 first mortgage at a 10 percent constant rate, which includes a 1 percent principal payback. The after-tax cash flow analysis for this property is shown in Figure 5.5.

Investment properties are expected to yield a satisfactory cash return on the investment (as shown by the after-tax cash flow in Figure 5.5) to ensure that the invested capital is not impaired and to present the opportunity for value enhancement. These are goals the owner will want to discuss with the manager when analyzing the cash flow statement and investigating economic alternatives to remedy unsatisfactory situations. If the cash return on the building in the example doesn't meet the owner's expectations for an acceptable return, the manager might suggest that the owner refinance the property, raise the rents, or institute strict cost-accounting procedures to reduce costs.

Reducing costs.   It is unwise to increase present cash flow by deferring expenditures for real maintenance needs. Savings may be made through volume buying or through an energy conservation program.

Final choices.   If rents are as high as the market will allow and costs are pared to the bone, but the property still does not show a satisfactory return, the owner is faced with four final choices: subsidize, make a major capital investment to increase the property's marketability, refinance to reduce debt service, or sell.

Figure 5.5 | After-Tax Cash Flow Analysis

After-Tax Cash Flow Analysis		
a. Gross annual income		$100,000
b. Operating costs ($50,000 – $5,000)		(45,000)
c. Net operating income (NOI)		$55,000
d. Capital expenditures		(5,000)
e. Debt service ($300,000 @ 10% constant)		
f. Interest payment		(27,000)
g. Principal (1% payback)		(3,000)
h. Income tax payable	$55,000	
Net operating income (c)	(27,000)	
Less interest payment (f)	(14,742)	
Less depreciation deduction*	$13,258	
$13,258 × 28% (tax bracket)		(3,712)
i. Net after-tax cash flow position		$16,288

Depreciation deduction	$400,000	Initial cost (Basis)
	+ 5,000	Capital expenditures
	$405,000	New basis
	× 0.0364	(See Chapter 9)
	$14,742	Annual depreciation deduction

■ Operating Budgets and Reports in Condos and Co-Ops

Condominium and cooperative managers must modify the financial reports used by apartment managers. They must prepare an annual operating budget, monthly income and expenditure statements, and yearly **cash flow reports.** However, the more complex system of ownership and the fact that the residents are also the owners create unique budgeting problems for condominiums and cooperatives. Because there is technically no income in a not-for-profit association, specialized training is a necessity for association managers.

Accurate Budget Projections

On the whole, many condominiums and cooperative suffer from a lack of long-range planning. Emphasis should be on managing for value rather than for profit. In budget projections, the manager must remember to make allowances for inflation and increasing rates, because the cost of all forms of energy continues to rise. **Reserve funds** should be budgeted for contingencies and replacement of major items such as roofs and central heating equipment. The amount should increase as the property ages and more repairs are needed. It is a disservice to the community as a whole to create inadequate budgets in response to pressure from the owners' association or to base any activity on internal political considerations.

Income. Condominium income comes almost entirely from assessments to members (owners of units), and income is budgeted to meet expenses.

Expenses. Most expenses relating to or arising from fee simple ownership of a unit are the sole responsibility of the owner. Some examples include utilities, interior decorating and maintenance, and so forth. However, in some condo projects, water supply and utilities for electricity, heating, and air-conditioning may not be metered separately to units. In that situation, a unit owner will pay a pro rata share of the total condominium expenses, including:

■ **Common elements.** The **common elements** include not only structural portions of a building but also common walkways, parking, and other areas for the use and benefit of all owners.

■ **Limited common elements.** Some condominiums establish limited common elements. These are areas such as porches, patios, or storage closets designated for the private use of the unit owner but not owned in fee simple as part of the unit itself.

■ **Calculating pro rata share.** An owner's pro rata share for each unit is determined by state statute and/or the ratio the square footage of the unit bears to the total square footage of all units in the project. It is expressed as a percentage, such as 1.034 percent. This percentage is established in the original condominium declaration (called *unit ownership declaration* in many states) and is the basis for allocating expenses applicable to all units.

■ **Capital expenditures.** If the need for an unbudgeted capital expenditure arises, a special assessment is necessary, which must be levied by a vote of either the board of directors of the association or the owners themselves, depending on the condominium declaration and bylaws.

■ Management Fees

When managing condominiums or cooperatives, there is a compelling reason why the management figure should be a flat fee rather than a percentage of gross income, as is generally used for residential apartment management. A percentage fee gives the residential manager incentive to raise rents and, thereby, gain extra profit. However, the revenue from cooperatives and condominiums comes not from rents. Condominium managers who contract for a percentage fee profit more by allowing **operating costs** to skyrocket, because this would increase the monthly assessments (total revenue) and, thereby, the percentage management fee. They can also profit, then, from increases in real property taxes and reserve funds.

Instead, condominium and cooperative management fees can be calculated using a cost-per-unit method or the management pricing worksheet. The **management pricing worksheet** relies on a per-unit cost method, with a slightly different approach. (See Figure 5.6.)

The worksheet is particularly useful when dealing with condominiums and cooperatives, groups that often insist on many long and tedious meetings with the various owners on the board of directors and the manager. By listing the various services provided and putting a value on those services, including meetings and travel time, the manager can more appropriately be compensated.

case study

Harriet Montgomery is the property manager of a large apartment complex for many years. One of the tenants, Han, came to Montgomery's office with a complaint. Han told Montgomery that his bathtub did not drain properly, but repeated requests to the resident manager, Fitzgerald, to have it repaired had been ignored. Han claimed that several of his friends, who are also tenants, had given Fitzgerald repair requests, and they had all been completed immediately. Han suspects that Fitzgerald is dragging his heels about his request because he is Asian American and Fitzgerald is discriminating against him.

Case Study Review

1. How should Harriet respond to Han's complaint?
    a. Reassure Han that she is sure that Fitzgerald would not discriminate against him
    b. Personally see that Han's repair is made in a timely manner
    c. Tell Fitzgerald to watch his back
    d. Write a note to herself to book some fair housing training one of these days

2. Harriet can institute all of the following to ward off similar complaints *EXCEPT*
    a. examine her office policies to make sure they comply with fair housing rules.
    b. institute training sessions on fair housing laws and bring up the topic regularly at staff meetings.
    c. ignore the issue because Han is the only person complaining.
    d. select someone in her office to be a compliance officer.

Figure 5.6 | Management Pricing Worksheet

Management Pricing

Property _____

No. of units _____300_____ Residents _____1,200_____ Offices _____1,200_____ Stores _____1,200_____ Boat slips _____

Age and present condition of property and improvements _____15 years old; good condition_____

_____

Miles from office _____20_____ Number of employees _____

Gross common area charge _____

Management/Leasing _____ Leasing _____

	No. Per Month	Hours Each	Total Hours	Cost
I. Property Supervisor's Services				
Inspections	1	6	6	$180.00
Site visits	1	4	4	120.00
Capital improvement supervision	–	–	–	–
Owner/Investor/Association meetings	1	2	2	60.00
Travel time: $ __30__ per hr. × __4__ hrs.			4	120.00
Office hours per month			10	300.00
Travel expense: __100 mi.__ × __33__ ¢ per mi.				33.00
Total				$813.00
II. Property Management Executive's Services				
Owner/Investor/Association meetings	1	2	2	$200.00
Site visits	–	–	–	–
Surveys and consultations	1	2	2	200.00
Inspections	1	4	4	400.00
Statement review	1	4	4	400.00
Budget preparation	–	–	–	–
Travel time: $ __50__ per hr. × __3__ hrs.			3	150.00
Travel expense: __75 mi.__ × __33__ ¢ per mi.				24.75
Total				$1,374.75
III. Accounting and Clerical Services				
Receipts accounted for: days per mo.	4	8	32	
Disbursements: invoices, payments	4	8	32	
Monthly billing	1	10	10	
Payroll: checks issued	2	8	16	
Owner/Assn. statement preparation	4	4	16	
Resident statement and preparation	50	1	50	
Statement duplication	10	2	20	
Owner consultation	–	–	–	
Total				$2,640.00
IV. Subtotal before Overhead and Profit				$4,827.75
V. Overhead and Profit		Percent of Total		
General overhead		10%		$483.00
Marketing		1%		48.00
Profit and contingencies		20%		966.00
VI. Total Monthly Fee				$6,324.75

$ _6,324.75_ Fee ÷ Units = $_____ each

Compiled by _____ **Approved** _____

■ Summary

Residential property may be broadly grouped into single-family residences, duplexes and triplexes, and apartments (commonly called multifamily dwellings).

Under cooperative ownership, a corporation or trust holds title to the property, and stockholders are granted proprietary leases that give them the right to occupy a unit of the building subject to rules and regulations. The purchaser in a condominium receives fee simple title to the unit, plus undivided common interest with the other residents in the common building elements and the land.

Federal laws set the standards. States and cities may add protections but may never take away protections offered by the federal law. The Civil Rights Act of 1866 is the oldest civil rights law and prohibits discrimination based on race or color in the sale or leasing of real and personal property. It was reaffirmed in 1968 by the *Jones v. Mayer* Supreme Court decision.

The Civil Rights Act of 1968, as amended, prohibits discrimination in the sale or rental of housing based on race, color, religion, national origin, sex, familial status, or disability. A tenant with a disability may modify the property to accommodate his or her disability, but he or she may be required to replace or repair those modifications at the end of the tenancy.

A manager may not deny housing to families unless the community is designated elderly (all older than 65) or near-elderly (80 percent are 55 and older). Discriminatory advertising is prohibited, and consistency in renting is expected without regard to the protected classes.

The property manager should constantly emphasize obedience of the law and remind staff that housing discrimination can result in large fines. At the very least, every office should prominently display the equal housing poster.

The property manager, who is not in daily contact with each building in his or her care, relies heavily on maintenance reports from the resident manager. These reports should cover not only surface maintenance but also upkeep of the building's vital plumbing and heating and ventilating systems. The manager of a smaller property with little or no on-site staff should be versatile enough to make minor repairs without calling in expensive skilled labor.

The property manager informs the owner of the property's financial status through the monthly cash flow reports. Funds should be conservatively budgeted in four categories of expense: taxes, insurance, maintenance, and administration.

The manager's cash flow analysis enables the owner to evaluate the return on the property investment. If the owner is dissatisfied, the property manager should suggest alternatives to the current management program. The after-tax cash flow on a property can sometimes be improved by an energy conservation program or other techniques for reducing operating expenses. In other cases, the property might have to be refinanced, altered, or even sold.

The managers of alternative forms of multifamily ownership such as cooperatives and condominiums work for a group of owner-occupants who have slightly different goals than either apartment building owners or tenants. These managers must be concerned primarily with maintaining the physical integrity of the premises and achieving the mutual goals of the owners, and the manager has no responsibility for occupancy levels.

Financial reports for cooperatives and condominiums are basically modified versions of those used for apartment buildings. Either the per-unit method of computing management fees or the management pricing worksheet can be included for co-ops and condos. Additional charges should be included for the extra time involved in communicating with and satisfying multiple owners.

■ Review Questions

True-False

1. The principles that apply to managing apartment buildings do not generally apply to managing other types of residential housing.
   a. True
   b. False

2. Management of single-family homes may not be as profitable as managing buildings.
   a. True
   b. False

3. The occupant of a condominium unit is a shareholder in a corporation that owns the underlying real property.
   a. True
   b. False

4. Individual ownership of an apartment, coupled with undivided common ownership of common areas, is characteristic of a cooperative.
   a. True
   b. False

5. A property manager is well advised to insist on long-term contracts with condominium boards in order to protect his or her interests.
   a. True
   b. False

6. Fair housing laws are designed to guarantee everyone an equal opportunity to live wherever they choose.
   a. True
   b. False

7. While a property manager would violate fair housing laws by steering prospective tenants to buildings in different parts of town, it is legal to designate certain areas of a single building or complex as set aside for members of a particular ethnic background or family structure.
   a. True
   b. False

8. Gross annual income – Operating costs = Net operating income.
   a. True
   b. False

9. One of the best ways to increase present cash flow is to defer expenditures for maintenance.
   a. True
   b. False

10. A condominium owner's pro rata share for his or her unit is determined by the ratio the square footage of the unit bears to the total square footage of all units in the project.
    a. True
    b. False

Multiple-Choice

1. What is the major difference between managing scattered-site housing and apartment buildings?
   a. There is no difference.
   b. Geography and time are factors that differ for each.
   c. Single-family homes are centralized.
   d. Repair costs for apartments are less.

2. Surveys of comparable properties and economic conditions are part of the
   a. building analysis.
   b. economic analysis.
   c. market analysis.
   d. management analysis.

3. Which is a special consideration when managing duplexes and triplexes?
   a. Showings to prospective tenants do not require many trips to the property.
   b. Tenants should have a high degree of compatibility.
   c. Return on investment is quite high.
   d. Repairs do not require much management time.

4. Unlike a manager of an investor-owned apartment building, the manager of a cooperative or condominium has no responsibility for maintaining
   a. occupancy levels.
   b. common areas.
   c. communication with the owners.
   d. administrative functions.

5. In managing condominiums and cooperatives, emphasis is on managing for
   a. value.
   b. profit.
   c. the short term.
   d. absentee owners.

6. Condominium and cooperative managers generally use the same financial reporting system as that used by
   a. certified public accountants.
   b. treasurers of corporations.
   c. managers of apartment buildings.
   d. owners of single-family homes.

7. The management fee for a condominium generally is
   a. prorated among the occupants according to their interests in the property.
   b. prorated among owners according to the square footage of each unit.
   c. expressed as a percentage of collected rents.
   d. a flat fee based on the costs of managing the property.

8. Whether to hire full-time or contract services for maintenance depends on
   a. hourly rates in the area.
   b. extent of benefits that must be added to salaries.
   c. whatever is most convenient for the manager.
   d. services required and cost-effectiveness to the owner.

9. Additional income can be derived from all of the following sources *EXCEPT*
   a. selling tenant insurance.
   b. vending machines.
   c. parking fees.
   d. Laundromat availability.

10. Whether to subsidize the building, sell out, or make a major improvement is a decision the owner must make after studying the
    a. five-year forecast.
    b. operating budget.
    c. management pricing worksheet.
    d. cash flow analysis.

11. A property manager had two vacancies. When a single parent and her child inquired about an apartment, they were told that the building was 100 percent occupied. This is an example of
    a. steering.
    b. blockbusting.
    c. redlining.
    d. a sound business practice.

12. If someone is found guilty of violating the Fair Housing Act of 1968, he or she may be liable for actual damages and maximum punitive damages of
    a. $11,000.
    b. $27,500.
    c. $55,000.
    d. an unlimited amount.

13. To avoid any allegations of illegal discrimination, the property manager should do all of the following *EXCEPT*
    a. prominently display the equal housing poster.
    b. develop a written fair housing policy affirming the commitment to equal housing opportunity.
    c. ensure that tenant selection is made based on the applicant's race or religion.
    d. provide fair housing training for all employees.

14. Of the following personnel, who is the "eyes and ears" of management at the actual property?
    a. Leasing agent
    b. Resident manager
    c. Bookkeeper
    d. Janitor

15. Although cash flow projections appear to be complex, they
    a. are based on figures from the data already gathered.
    b. can be prepared by the property manager with the owner's assistance.
    c. are simple in design and do not contribute to the owner's decision making.
    d. are not complex, because they have no impact on tax returns.

chapter six

Managing Risk and Tenant Safety Issues

■ Key Terms

asbestos	hazardous waste	radon
carbon monoxide	lead-based paint	risk management
flood insurance	life safety officer (LSO)	tenant emergency
hazardous substance	mold	procedures manual
		tenant wardens

learning objectives

On completing this chapter, you will be able to

■ identify four methods of risk management and the implications of each—avoid, control, retain, or transfer the risk;

■ list types of insurance that the owner, property manager, and tenants should carry;

■ differentiate between hazardous materials and hazardous waste;

■ name several environmental hazards and describe ways that the property manager can minimize their effects;

■ describe components of a life safety program utilizing personnel, equipment, and procedures to reach four important goals: preventing an emergency, detecting a breach, containing the damage, and counteracting the damage; and

■ discuss the importance of preventing criminal activity on the property.

■ Risk Management

Environmental concerns require an increasing amount of management time and attention and may affect the availability of insurance as well, especially regarding mold-related claims and flood insurance. The property manager may manage structures containing hazardous materials, and if these are produced by the manager's employer or tenants, the manager must see that they are properly disposed of. In areas where recycling is becoming the norm, the property manager must provide recycling facilities and see that tenants sort their trash properly.

Risk Management and Insurance

One of the most critical areas of responsibility for a property manager, because of the potentially great dollar and personal losses, is the field of risk management and insurance. The property manager should have a working knowledge of casualty, liability, and special lines of insurance.

Liability Alert!

The Insurance Decision

Although the property owner may consult the property manger, the final decision about any property insurance should be made by the owner after consulting with his or her own insurance agent.

Risk management theories.   Risk management principles can be examined and implemented in the following ways:

■ Identifying the risk and measuring its frequency and financial severity

■ Avoiding the risk or discontinuing the loss-causing activity

■ Controlling the risk with safety programs, loss reduction plans, and emergency preparedness

■ Retaining the risk and internally funding loss consequences

■ Transferring the risk to insurers or to third parties

■ Monitoring the results and ongoing fit of the risk management strategies implemented

Property manager as a claims adjuster.   The objective in any claim settlement is to compensate the owner for damages suffered in accordance with the terms and conditions of the insurance policies. For serious damage, the renter or property manager should call in the claim as soon as possible and take pictures of the damage. Either or both should arrange for temporary repairs to prevent additional damage, keeping all receipts. The property owner should be notified as soon as possible.

Types of Insurance

The property owner and manager are both exposed to the consequences of loss or accidents and need the protection offered by various types of insurance.

Insurable interest.   One can buy insurance only on something or someone that he or she has a reason to be involved with. For example, the owner of the building can buy insurance to cover the building in case of a loss, but the tenants must purchase their own insurance to cover what belongs to them.

Owner's hazard insurance policies.   As a representative of the policy buyer, the property manager must determine the risks involved, shop the market for the best and most economical coverage, and then purchase the required policies on behalf of the owner. The property manager should consider several insurance coverages.

At a minimum, considerations should include the following:

■ Property insurance, including fire, lightning, windstorm, vandalism, and malicious mischief

■ Flood insurance

■ Loss of income following damage to structures or their contents

■ Additional costs for temporary premises that are required following a loss

■ Rental value of leased premises that must be replaced by more expensive leases

■ Workers' compensation and employers' liability for injury to works

■ Commercial automobile liability, including hired and nonowned automobiles, to cover injury and damage by vehicles

■ Commercial general liability, including liability for contractors, completed operations, product, and contractually assumed liabilities

Flood insurance.   No homeowners', renters', or building insurance policies cover water damage as a result of rising waters, nor can an endorsement be added. The policies must be purchased separately and subsidized policies are available to any property owner located in a community participating in the National Flood Insurance Program (NFIP).

Insurance for the tenant.   As a standard practice, the property manager should notify, in writing, all tenants—residential, commercial, and industrial— that they must obtain renters' insurance to protect their personal belongings. It may help to explain *insurable interest*, stating that the landlord cannot buy coverage if he or she does not own the property.

Insurance for the manager.   The manager, as both a custodian and a contracting businessperson, may hire employees or contractors; handle client funds, documents, and records; and maintain an office and files. The manager should insure office contents, equipment, supplies, and computers and software.

The manager should also purchase employee dishonesty insurance to cover money, merchandise, and any other property for which the manager may be held accountable. The manager should also carry *errors and omissions insurance* (with limits of at least 10 percent of the total annual collections) to protect against possible accounting mistakes or other oversights, including *failure to act*.

Liability Alert!

Monitor Insurance Coverage

Constant vigilance of insurance certificates on the part of owners, their subcontractors, and tenants is a vital part of risk management. The property manager should set up ongoing compliance suspense files.

■ Managing Environmental Issues

Managers must work to ensure the health and safety of their own employees and their tenants and for the community at large.

Typical Hazardous Substances

Although the terms *hazardous substances* and *hazardous waste* are often used interchangeably, they are not synonymous. A **hazardous waste** is generally a by-product of a manufactured item that itself may not be subject to environmental law or regulation. A **hazardous substance,** however, is broader in scope and may include everyday items such as household cleaning products and paint.

The property manager should be aware of the following typical hazardous substances:

- **Mold**. Molds are biological pollutants that require a cellulosic food source and moisture to grow. Since the number one prevention technique is moisture control, managers should encourage tenants to immediately report any water intrusion. Managers should document all maintenance procedures.

- **Asbestos.** Asbestos management and control was an important concern for commercial property managers in the 1990s but is lessening today. Asbestos-containing material (ACM), applied by spray as a surfacing, fireproofing, and insulating material, is present in many public and private buildings throughout the country. Several actions can be taken to manage asbestos: encapsulation, enclosure, and removal, which is the most drastic and most expensive.

- **Radon.** Radon is an invisible, odorless, and tasteless radioactive gas that occurs naturally and has been linked to lung cancer. Of all the environmental risks, radon is the easiest to mitigate by sealing the property and installing PVC pipes. A fan at the top of the PVC pipe will "suck up" vapors in the soil, including radon, and then disburse them outside.

- **Carbon monoxide.** Carbon monoxide (CO), a colorless, odorless, tasteless gas, is one of the most common and deadly poisons in our environment. CO is a by-product of incomplete burning of fossil fuels. Many problems arise when tenants use portable space heaters without adequate ventilation. Whole apartment and office buildings have been sickened by faulty water heaters and inadequately vented furnaces. Even if not required by law, landlords and property managers should install CO detectors in every rental unit and test them monthly according to the manufacturer's instructions.

- **Chlorofluorocarbons (CFCs).** Chlorofluorocarbons (CFCs, or Freon™) are manmade, inert, nontoxic, nonflammable chemical gases used primarily as refrigerants in motor vehicle air conditioners (MVACs), building air-conditioning units, refrigerators, and freezers. A single molecule of CFC can destroy 100,000 molecules of ozone. The property manager should consider upgrading the appliances to use the newer, environmentally friendly products. All appliances, such as air-conditioning units and refrigerators, must be properly disposed of.

- **Lead-based paint.** Lead is a heavy, soft, malleable, blue-gray metal found as a natural ore and/or as a by-product of smelting silver. Once removed from the ground, it is part of man's environment forever. At the present time, there is no known way to render lead harmless. Although high concentrations will affect anyone, children under the age of six are particularly vulnerable.

- **Lead-Based Paint Hazard Reduction Act.** Managers of any residential property built before 1978, with only a few exceptions, are required to do the following:

  - Disclose to the tenant the presence of any known lead-based paint or hazards

  - Provide tenants with copies of any available records or reports pertaining to the presence of lead-based paint and/or hazards; completed disclosures must be retained for three years

  - Give the tenant a copy of the EPA lead hazard information pamphlet, "Protecting Your Family from Lead in Your Home," which is available from *www.epa.gov* in several languages

  - Protect both workers and tenants from exposure to lead-based paint contaminated dust while work is being done

---

Liability Alert!

Get the Lead-based Paint Forms Signed and Stored

There are 11 possible violations per lease. Failure to comply with these regulations could result in civil fines from $110 to $11,000 per violation, in addition to any criminal fines and awards of triple damages that may be assessed.

■ Managing Life Safety and Security

The management of life safety and security is a special management concern that is increasingly becoming more complex and sophisticated. We no longer think solely in terms of *security* for office buildings, shopping centers, and other properties, but instead in terms of the total environment and the protection of those in that environment from harm caused by criminal acts, natural disasters, and hazardous materials.

Building security no longer simply means the presence of a night watchman. Security is a 24/7 responsibility, and the modern approach to dealing with emergencies such as fire and natural disasters focuses on prevention and safety. Hence, the term *life safety* has come into favor.

Life Safety Officers

Security officers are now called **life safety officers (LSOs).** Their responsibilities have increased commensurably with technical advances and the changing needs of property owners. Generally, a good life safety and security program is a three-pronged approach that incorporates skilled use of equipment, personnel, and procedure. Such a program is based on four goals:

1. *Preventing* emergencies or security breaches
2. *Detecting* a breach as early as possible and sounding an alarm
3. *Containing* or confining the damage or intrusion as much as possible
4. *Counteracting* the damage by prompt and proper action

Emergency Equipment and Technologies

Modern security technology is available in the form of advanced electronic equipment (intercommunication networks, automated fire protection and security systems, access control, and closed-circuit television), which in many buildings is integrated with lighting and temperature control devices. The property manager must plan carefully to coordinate all of these elements into an effective integrated system; individual features must be selected with care and then fitted into the overall system.

While new buildings are constructed with state-of-the-art electronic devices, property managers of older structures must retrofit their buildings to provide these same services. Retrofitting is more expensive, so often it is best done on a phase-by-phase basis.

Building Systems

The design concept of present-day emergency equipment is to discover and report a fire or other emergency before it further threatens life and property. The focal point of up-to-date emergency response systems is a master central control panel in a life safety control room that automatically monitors smoke detectors, water flow switches for the sprinkler system, and manual fire alarm pull stations located throughout the building.

Telephones or telephone jacks should be located next to each exit door and in the elevator lobbies for intercommunication between the floor of the emergency and the control room. These communication devices are useful to firefighters, maintenance personnel, and security staff.

Elevators.   The danger in using elevators during a building fire comes from heat and smoke or toxic gases accumulated in the elevator shaft. Elevator shafts running throughout the building create a chimney effect, causing an updraft of air and filling them with smoke, which can be poisonous to elevator occupants.

Liability Alert!

Anticipate the Needs of Disabled Tenants

Provisions must be made to evacuate physically impaired persons from floors affected by emergencies. Thus, a life safety officer or someone especially designated must capture an elevator and take it to a safe floor closest to the fire. Responding personnel must then disencumber the disabled person from wheelchair or crutches and carry the individual down the stairwell to a waiting elevator or safe location.

Smoke detectors.   Smoke detectors, which will indicate danger by flashing a light on the detector housing panel, should be located on each floor. In a centralized system, a charged smoke detector will prompt a local alarm or an alarm in the fire control room. Although smoke detectors usually reset automatically once they have been cleared of smoke, the manager should ensure that the detectors are tested regularly.

Sprinkler system.   Water flow detectors signal the fire panel when a sprinkler head is discharging water, a pipe has broker, or another plumbing malfunction has occurred. Sprinkler water flow switches reset automatically when water ceases to flow through the system.

■ Role of Personnel in Life Safety

The first priority of a life safety and security program is the protection of human life. During an emergency, members of the building staff will be expected to help combat the danger and protect human life, but under no circumstances must any person undertake unnecessary risks that would endanger themselves or other building occupants. A life safety program is for the protection of all persons in the building, staff members included.

It is impossible to determine in advance exactly how an emergency will occur, so systems to mobilize, deploy, and protect personnel must be designed to provide a wide range of responses to any emergency. Each member of the building staff must be well informed about how the system works and the problems that may be encountered in handling an emergency.

Central Base of Operations

The key to dealing with all emergencies is to establish a central headquarters, or a base of operations. All communications should come from a designated person in the life safety control center. In buildings with small staffs, this may be the manager's office or the information desk. Large complexes establish an elaborate life safety control center, fully staffed 24 hours a day and usually located on the ground floor or on a floor below grade. Although the following discussion describes procedures for a larger complex, the manager of a smaller property should have no trouble adapting the principles to that property.

All building personnel who do not have specific emergency assignments should report to a central point for assignments, and all emergency personnel should be directed from a central location on ground level.

Personnel Assignments

The following descriptions of the roles played by various building personnel in an emergency assumes a sizable building staff available for assignment to life safety and security duties in addition to daily occupational routines. A person can be assigned more than one task.

The property manager and staff must be well trained and disciplined to act effectively and calmly; the tenants must respond to staff orders. Everyone must follow routines as set forth in planned procedures. Drills should be held periodically.

Emergency spokesperson. An authorized spokesperson should be designated in advance and must be available constantly to represent management on the scene and provide immediate factual information on personnel casualties to employees' families. This person is responsible for notifying the property owner as soon as possible.

Tenant wardens. Many tenants have skills or training that would be of critical assistance in an emergency. The property manager should locate and qualify these people through the tenant warden and through questionnaires, and they should be trained to effectively supplement building staff during emergencies.

Police department. Outside the building, pedestrian and automobile traffic is the responsibility of the police department. From a legal standpoint, official emergency crews are in control as soon as they enter the building.

■ Property Management Procedures

Each property manager is charged with the development and implementation of procedures that emphasize employee training, fire and accident prevention, good housekeeping, equipment maintenance, and safety of tenants, customers, employees, and the community. Procedures must meet requirements of the Occupational Safety and Health Administration (OSHA) and other applicable laws.

Life Safety Procedures

Life safety procedures are usually organized under in-house (or internal) procedures and hazard detection and emergency evacuation procedures.

Internal procedures. These usually concern only building management and its employees. Procedures are circulated only on a need-to-know basis and are given only to that group.

Hazard detection. Newer buildings are equipped with state-of-the-art security, fire detection, and building operating systems, but older structures may not be. The latter may depend more on management procedures than on technology.

Disaster planning. A disaster procedure or emergency response plan calls for setting up an off-site command post and a chain of command. Prior arrangements must be made on a standby basis with suppliers of emergency items or necessary repair material.

Emergency supplies. If space and budget permit, it is good practice to stockpile a small quantity of emergency supplies. In a hurricane zone, for example, enough plywood could be kept on hand to board up all ground-floor windows. In an area subject to earthquakes or hurricanes, a 72-hour food and water supply might be maintained. Additionally, if a building does not have a standby or auxiliary electricity source, a generator with ample fuel supply should be kept available.

Evacuation drills. The tenant warden group should be involved in developing evacuation plans and practice drills. Buildings that are higher than the local fire department is equipped to reach—generally seven stories or above—may require more elaborate emergency evacuation planning and drills.

Emergency Preparedness Procedures

At a minimum, emergency response plans should include fire, explosion, severe weather, bomb threat, evacuation, and elevator emergency procedures. In certain areas, earthquake, tornado, hurricane, flooding, and blizzard plans may need to be prepared as well.

Liability Alert!

Develop Emergency Preparedness Procedures

Written procedures detailing emergency organization members' duties should be provided to each member and periodic training sessions held to test emergency response. Managers must develop and keep current emergency plans for their properties.

Inspection Procedures

Protection of company assets, tenants, and the general public depends on minimizing hazards at each property. Many potential emergencies can be detected and minimized by instituting a thorough life safety inspection procedure. Fire protection systems must be inspected on a regular basis and repairs made immediately. In addition, walk-through inspections for safety hazards and housekeeping problems should be conducted by building management at least twice annually, with more thorough inspections annually.

Liability Alert!

Inspection Procedures

Structural inspections should be a day-to-day practice of the maintenance technicians, and if defects are found, a structural engineer should be engaged to make an inspection. Documentation of all inspections should be retained in management files for a period of at least two years, along with documentation of repairs of defective or damaged equipment discovered during inspections.

Communicating with Tenants

In any building emergency—from a partially flooded floor due to a plumbing breakdown to a total conflagration—it is imperative that the property manager make immediate contact with each tenant. An open, sympathetic, and understanding manner is essential, and the property manager would do well to prepare a written statement that could be used as a guideline so that all points will be covered, particularly if he or she is unable to contact each tenant personally.

Tenants should be advised of the steps management is taking to handle the emergency, what reconstruction is planned, and any other item pertinent to the immediate situation. In cases of property damage, tenants should be requested to contact the insurers that cover their personal property and office equipment. Although the building insurance may take care of some damage, most leases provide that the landlord is not responsible under certain circumstances, and in these cases, the tenant's insurance coverage is critical.

Liability Alert!

Control Media Coverage of Emergencies

During an emergency, news media may seek access to the area to cover the event, and to the extent possible, the property manager should cooperate fully with media, authorities, and other segments of the public. Factual information should be provided as quickly as facts can be verified. However, permitting unlimited media access to damaged areas may compromise insurance inspections and the work of police or fire investigators. Admissions of liability or speculations about the cause of an accident or damage to property of others should be avoided, and no estimates of the extent of the damage or the amount of reconstruction costs should be made until they can be accurately assessed.

Tenant Emergency Procedures Manual

The property manager should make a printed **tenant emergency procedures manual** available to tenants. The booklet should include procedures for the following emergency situations:

- Accident or illness
- Tornado or hurricane
- Earthquake
- Fire drill
- Bomb threat
- Elevator emergencies (including building or floor evacuation and special emergencies)

Minimizing Post-Emergency Damage

The first consideration after a disaster has damaged a building is the safety of personnel who may need to gain access to the premises. A structural engineer should be immediately engaged, together with the assistance of the fire department and building code enforcement officials, to determine just how safe the damaged structure is and what sort of access can be allowed. It is in the best interest of the owner for the property manager to take immediate steps to prevent further damage, not only to prevent further loss but also to meet insurance requirements.

Liability Alert!

Be Aware of Insurance Requirements

Insurance policies often provide reimbursement to the owner for expenses incurred to prevent loss beyond initial damage, over and above the amounts payable for the damage itself. However, the property manager must be aware that if additional damage occurs that reasonably could have been prevented, the insurer will not pay.

Disaster Aftershocks

Business interruption insurance is designed to alleviate financial losses from suspension of rent. It is very simple to compute lost rent, but the dollars-and-cents effect of collateral costs, such as the loss of customers, is intangible and thus difficult to measure and quantify. Many fallout costs may not be recoverable from insurance.

Losses from business interruption, however, are best reduced by resuming operation as soon as possible. In the event of a widespread catastrophe, these reconstruction specialists will be in high demand, so having prior acquaintance with these contractors and contingent arrangements for their services should ensure their availability if disaster strikes.

■ Criminal Activity Issues

A critical safety issue is protection from criminal acts. Crime has recently become the number one problem for many Americans, and certainly for many property managers. In fact, homicide has become the second leading cause of death across the nation. Homicide is the leading cause of death for women in the workplace.

Liability Alert!

Managers May Be Liable for Criminal Acts

Property owners and managers are increasingly being held accountable for third parties' criminal acts against their tenants. For example, a shopping center owner in Los Angeles was ordered to pay $3.5 million to the parents of four teenage girls who were murdered during a robbery in a store where two of the girls worked. Property managers may reduce their liability by making sure the premises they manage are as secure as possible.

Hiring Security Personnel

Property managers may choose to hire their own security personnel or contract with a security firm. If property managers hire their own personnel, they must take special care to properly train and supervise those personnel.

In order to choose a competent security firm, a property manager must have clearly defined standards and then carefully evaluate the quality of the services offered. The manager must decide what duties are required of the security personnel, what equipment is needed, who will provide the insurance coverage, and who will provide supplies, such as uniforms. The manager must carefully screen the firms by thoroughly checking all references and investigating their hiring, training, and supervision policies.

Potentially Hazardous Locations

Some areas of a property are more susceptible to criminal activity and require extra care. The parking lots of shopping centers, for example, are prime locations for criminal and gang activity. Landscaping should not provide hiding places near cars or obscure walkways; lighting should be improved to increase customer confidence; the number of patrol vehicles should be increased; patrol vehicles can be made more visible with brightly colored markings; and customer service booths can be installed at strategic places in the parking lot. Closed-circuit television systems allow security personnel to monitor isolated places where crimes are more likely to occur.

Employee Crime

Property managers can be held liable for any crimes committed by their employees, based on the argument that the property manager made an improper hiring decision. To minimize this liability, property managers should thoroughly screen job applicants. After hiring all personnel, the property manager must carefully supervise them: property managers should never allow employees to engage in conduct that endangers others. If a property manager learns that an employee is behaving recklessly or criminally, corrective action should be taken immediately.

Liability Alert!

Limit Liability through Lease Clauses

While landlords cannot be completely protected from liability for injuries and damages caused by crime, lease provisions can be used to minimize liability. Property managers should consult competent, experienced attorneys to determine if their standard lease clauses should be changed to help protect themselves and property owners from excessive liability.

---

case study

Susan Kim manages a small business park in a normally quiet suburban location. Recently, however, several of the major tenants have been complaining about a crime wave. Several businesses have been burglarized, and one tenant's employee was mugged in the parking lot. Also, the local newspaper has published several articles on the increased danger of flooding in the area, due to increased building in the nearby watershed. Tenants have asked Susan Kim to increase security, reduce crime, and develop an emergency plan in the event that the business park floods next spring.

Case Study Review

1. What should Susan do first?
    a. Contact an engineer about the flooding problem
    b. Buy more flood insurance for her tenants
    c. Organize a neighborhood watch program
    d. Hire a security firm

2. What should Susan do next?
    a. Tell the tenants to clean up the parking lot and to install more lighting
    b. Complain to the municipal authorities about the flooding issue
    c. Develop procedures to follow in the event of any type of emergency
    d. Sell business protection insurance to her tenants

■ Summary

One of the major concerns of a property owner is obtaining insurance coverage against as many risks as possible at the most reasonable rate. As risk managers for the owner, property managers examine potential risks to see which should be avoided, retained, controlled, and transferred through the purchase of insurance. They may be called on to adjust claims for insured property losses. While property managers may advise the owners, a final insurance decision should be made by the owner after consulting with his or her own insurance broker.

Managers must address environmental issues, including radon, mold, asbestos, carbon monoxide, and lead-based paint. Managers of all residential properties built before 1978 must properly notify their tenants of the potential hazards of lead-based paint. The manager must use the forms developed by the EPA and retain the completed disclosures for three years.

A life safety plan should be based on four goals: prevention, detection of the problem and sounding an alarm, containment of damage, and counteraction of damage. The property manager should designate specific responsibilities to all building staff. Trained tenant wardens and preselected tenants who possess useful skills or training should assist with the care and evacuation of occupants.

During a building emergency, it is imperative that the property manager make immediate individual contact to advise each tenant of the crisis and how it is being handled. A second priority is to cooperate with the news media authorities and the public, while retaining the control necessary to deal with the emergency.

An emergency-procedures guide, distributed to all tenants, should outline emergency response plans for accident or illness, severe weather, fire, bomb threats, and elevator problems. Following a disaster, the property manager must concentrate on preventing further damage and minimizing the loss. Resuming normal operations as quickly as possible is the best way to keep business losses at a minimum.

More and well-trained security personnel and security devices can be used to increase safety and decrease criminal activity. Property managers must be especially careful to watch for and work to eliminate illegal activities on the property.

■ Review Questions

True-False

1. Building security can be effectively and economically addressed simply by hiring a night security guard.
   a. True
   b. False

2. The four goals of a life safety and security program are prevention, detection, containment, and counteraction.
   a. True
   b. False

3. The owner of the property is responsible for purchasing insurance to cover the tenant's property.
   a. True
   b. False

4. Molds require a cellulosic food source, moisture, and sunlight in order to grow.
   a. True
   b. False

5. The first priority of any safety and security program is the preservation of the property's value.
   a. True
   b. False

6. A property manager must relinquish authority over an emergency situation to official emergency crews as soon as they enter the building.
   a. True
   b. False

7. Flood insurance is always a separate insurance policy.
   a. True
   b. False

8. During a building emergency, the best response to media inquiries is to refuse to comment.
   a. True
   b. False

9. It is advisable to put together a printed emergency procedures manual for tenants.
   a. True
   b. False

10. Owners may buy insurance to transfer their risk.
    a. True
    b. False

Multiple-Choice

1. Safety programs coupled with loss reduction plans and emergency preparedness are examples of
   a. avoiding the risk.
   b. retaining the risk.
   c. transferring the risk.
   d. controlling the risk.

2. Shifting risk in part or wholly to insurers is an example of
   a. avoiding the risk.
   b. retaining the risk.
   c. transferring the risk.
   d. controlling the risk.

3. Which coverage must always be purchased as a separate policy from the standard owners' multiperil insurance policy?
   a. Fire
   b. Windstorm
   c. Loss of income
   d. Flood

4. Which pollutant is caused by faulty water heaters and inadequately vented furnaces?
   a. Carbon monoxide
   b. Radon
   c. Mold
   d. Chlorofluorocarbons

5. Many commercial managers have had to supervise the removal of
   a. radon.
   b. formaldehyde.
   c. PCBs.
   d. asbestos.

6. Disclosures must be made to tenants about the potential problems with lead-based paint in any residential rental constructed
   a. before 1900.
   b. prior to 1978.
   c. after 1978.
   d. after 1996.

7. An odorless, invisible, and tasteless gas that occurs naturally in the environment that has been linked to lung cancer is
   a. radon.
   b. formaldehyde.
   c. carbon monoxide.
   d. mold.

8. To meet federal requirements, how long should a property manager retain copies of the lead-based hazard disclosure statements?
   a. Indefinitely
   b. Three years
   c. Five years
   d. Seven years

9. What type of insurance can protect a property manager from possible accounting mistakes or other oversights?
   a. Errors and omissions insurance
   b. Employee dishonesty insurance
   c. Workers' compensation
   d. Business liability insurance

10. A good life safety and security program will include
    a. skilled use of equipment.
    b. skilled personnel.
    c. good procedures.
    d. all of the above.

11. The first priority of a life safety and security program is the protection of the
    a. property.
    b. human life.
    c. security staff.
    d. reputation of the owner.

12. The person who has the responsibility to assist in tenant evacuation as well as enforce safety measures is the
    a. life safety officer.
    b. emergency spokesperson.
    c. life safety control center operator.
    d. property manager.

13. One way to work toward controlling illegal activities is to
    a. ignore maintenance needs.
    b. not involve other tenants.
    c. ignore employee crime.
    d. make improvements to potentially hazardous locations.

14. In any building emergency, the property manager should first
    a. file an insurance claim.
    b. alert the newspapers.
    c. call the police.
    d. contact each tenant.

15. After a disaster, owners and managers should
    a. wait until the insurance adjuster arrives before making attempts to secure the property.
    b. take pictures and secure the property.
    c. call the insurance company for specific instructions.
    d. contact the tenants to let them know that rent is still due.

agent An individual who is legally empowered to act on behalf of another.

Americans with Disabilities Act (ADA) A federal law that requires that property open to the public includes features that facilitate access to the building. The ADA is designed to eliminate discrimination against individuals with disabilities by providing equal access to jobs, public accommodations, government services, public transportation, and telecommunications.

antitrust laws Laws designed to preserve free enterprise of the open marketplace by making illegal certain private conspiracies and combinations formed to minimize competition. Most violations of antitrust laws in the real estate business involve either *price-fixing* (brokers or managers agreeing to set fixed compensation rates) or *allocation of customers or services* (brokers or managers agreeing to limit their areas of trade or dealing to certain areas or properties).

asbestos A mineral fiber, classified as a carcinogen. Found in asbestos-containing materials, it was used in older properties in insulation, shingles, siding, concrete, floor and ceiling tiles, plasters, and more.

asset management services The assembly, management, and disposition of a portfolio of investment properties.

assignment Transfer of a tenant's remaining rental rights in a property to a third party. The tenant can transfer rights but not responsibilities unless agreed to by the landlord.

blockbusting The illegal practice of inducing homeowners to sell or apartment dwellers to move out by making representations regarding the entry or prospective entry of persons of a particular race or national origin into the neighborhood. Sometimes referred to as *panic selling.*

carbon monoxide An air pollutant that is a colorless, odorless, poisonous gas that is a by-product of incomplete combustion of burning fossil fuels, such as gasoline, kerosene, wood, and oil.

cash flow The amount of money available for use after paying expenses and the debt service (the mortgage).

cash flow report A financial report showing the property's net operating income minus all additional disbursements such as debt service and capital improvements and the amount remitted to the owner.

Civil Rights Act of 1866 A federal law that guarantees that citizens of all races have the same rights as white citizens to inherit, purchase, lease, sell, hold, and convey real and personal property. Reaffirmed by the *Jones V. Mayer* Supreme Court decision in 1968.

Civil Rights Act of 1968 Federal law, Title VIII, often called the Fair Housing Act, that prohibits discrimination in the sale, rental, or financing of housing based on race, color, religion, national origin, familial status, and disability.

commercial property Income-producing properties; public accommodations.

commingling Combining client funds with the property manager's business or personal funds.

common elements Parts of a property that are necessary or convenient to the existence, maintenance, and safety of a condominium, or that are normally in common use by all of the condominium residents. Each condominium owner has an undivided ownership interest in the common elements.

comparative income and expense analysis An estimate of the cost of improvements, alterations, or remodeling that are consistent with the owner's objectives and are needed to command optimum rentals.

concierge services A trend in the property management field that provides personal, secretarial, catering, or other services to the occupants of office or residential buildings.

condominium A form of property ownership in which each occupant of a multiunit building owns his or her dwelling unit separately and an undivided interest with other owners in the property's common elements (lobbies, hallways, etc.).

constructive eviction A situation in which a tenant must abandon the premises because of the landlord's negligence in providing essential services.

contraction Part of an economic cycle in which economic activity decreases.

cooperative A residential multifamily building whose title is held by a trust or corporation that is owned by and operated for the benefit of persons living within the building, who are the beneficial owners of the trust or stockholders of the corporation, each possessing a proprietary lease that gives them the right to occupy a certain unit in the building.

covenants, conditions, and restrictions (CC&Rs) A set of private restrictions on the use of a specific parcel of real property; often used with a condominium development.

disability Any physical or mental impairment that substantially limits one or more of an individual's major life activities, including caring for oneself, performing manual tasks, walking, seeing, hearing, speaking, and working. Persons with AIDS are protected by the fair housing laws under this classification, as those participating in addiction recovery programs, but current users of illegal drugs are not.

duplex Two-apartment building.

employee A worker whose work is directed and controlled by the person for whom he or she works. The employer controls when, where, and how the work is done as well as defines the desired end result of the work. Usually the employer withholds taxes and pays a portion of the employee's contribution into the Social Security retirement fund.

employer The individual or company who pays people to work for them. State laws determine the minimum number of persons hired, total amount of wages paid, and working conditions that must exist to classify as an employer.

Equal Credit Opportunity Act (ECOA) The federal law passed to protect borrowers when applying for a loan. The lender (or property manager) can deny a borrower credit based only on reasonable business reasons, not because of the borrower's race, color, religion, national origin, receipt of public assistance, age, or marital status.

equal housing logo A picture of a house containing an equal sign. This logo should be included in all display ads, brochures, and other forms of advertising, indicating to the public that the landlord/manager will not discriminate against individuals based on their race, color, religion, national origin, sex, familial status, or handicap.

escalation clause A lease clause providing that the rental rate will increase or decrease according to a selected index of economic conditions, such as the consumer price index.

estate for years A leasehold estate that continues for a specified period of time. It is not ordinarily terminated by death of either party or by the sale of the property.

estate from period to period A leasehold estate that is automatically renewed for successive periods of time until either party gives notice to the other.

eviction notice A landlord's legal notice to a tenant explaining the tenant's default under the terms of the lease and informing him or her of a pending eviction suit.

expansion Part of the economic cycle in which the economy grows.

Fair Housing Act (Title VIII of the Civil Rights Act of 1968) The federal law that prohibits discrimination in the sale, rental, or financing of housing based on race, color, religion, national origin, sex, familial status, and disability.

familial status A class of people protected by the federal Fair Housing Act, which is defined as the presence of at least one individual in the family who is younger than 18 or the presence of a pregnant woman.

fiduciary duties The duties of an agent to the principal to maintain the greatest trust and confidence, generally including the duties of care, obedience of lawful instructions, accountability, loyalty, and disclosure of material facts.

five-year forecast A long-term projection of estimated expenditures and income based on predictable changes.

flood insurance Insurance that compensates for physical damage resulting from flooding. Rising water damage usually is not covered by other insurance and generally must be purchased separately.

general agent An agent who can act on behalf of the principal on a range of matters and can obligate the principal to any contracts signed by the agent that are within the scope of that agent's duties.

gross collectible rental income The estimated revenue after deducting the percentage of probable rent loss resulting from vacancies, tenant defaults on leases, and tenant turnover.

gross lease A common residential lease under which the tenant pays a fixed rental and the landlords pays all of the operating expenses for the property.

hazardous substance Any material designated by the EPA to be a threat to human health and/or the environment, often including products that are ignitable, corrosive, toxic, or explosive.

hazardous waste Solid wastes that have been listed by the EPA and are ignitable, corrosive, toxic, or reactive.

incubator space A building located in an industrial park and divided into small units of varying sizes to accommodate young, growing companies that want to combine office and industrial space at one location.

index lease A lease containing an escalation clause that is tied to an index.

industrial property The type of property that converts raw materials into finished products for storage and distribution of goods.

lead-based paint Paint often used in homes built prior to 1978 that contains lead, a mineral that made the paint shiny and durable. There is no known method to render lead harmless after it has been removed from the earth.

Lead-Based Paint Hazard Reduction Act (LBPHRA) The federal act that seeks to control exposure to lead-based paint hazards, specifically mentioning protecting children younger than six. It requires that landlords of properties built before 1978 make certain disclosures before entering into a lease.

lease A written or oral contract between a landlord (lessor) and a tenant (lessee) that transfers the right to exclusive possession and use of the landlord's real property to the lessee for a specified period of time and for a stated consideration (rent). Most state laws require that leases over more than a certain amount of time must be in writing to be enforceable.

leasehold estate A tenant's right to occupy real estate for a specified period of time in exchange for some form of compensation.

leasing agent Salespeople who are skilled in communications and telephone techniques, on-site customer qualifying, merchandising themselves and their properties, and closing techniques.

life safety officer (LSO) The person who, in the event of an emergency, is responsible for assisting tenant evacuation and enforcing safety precautions.

management contract The contract between an income property owner (principal) and a management firm or individual property manager (agent) that outlines the scope of the manager's authority, owner's responsibilities, and compensation.

management plan The financial and operational strategy for the ongoing management of a property.

management pricing worksheet A method of computing management fees by itemizing management activities, calculating the direct cost to the firm, and adding a percentage for profit. This method is most appropriate when managing condominium communities.

manufactured home park A popular, expanding form of residential living consisting of permanently or semipermanently situated manufactured homes. The ground only, the home, or both may be rented from the owner.

market An exchange of goods and services between willing sellers and willing buyers.

market analysis An analysis that integrates information about the specific, local area where the property is located.

Megan's law Federal and state laws requiring that certain sex offenders register with local law enforcement agencies.

ministorage facilities Small, secure storage units rented to individuals and small businesses.

mold Simple, microscropic living organisms that exist both indoors and outdoors and that require a food source and moisture to thrive. An indoor air quality issue because they produce airborne spores that may be toxic or cause allergic reactions and respiratory symptoms in some people.

net lease A common industrial lease form requiring the tenant to pay rent plus certain costs incurred in the operation of the property. Generally, straight net leases require the tenant to pay rent, utilities, real estate taxes, and assessments. Net-net leases require the tenant to pay rent, utilities, real estate taxes, assessment, and insurance premiums. Net-net-net, or triple-net, leases may require the tenant to pay all of the above expenses plus agreed-on items of maintenance and repair.

office property A type of income-producing commercial property from which a particular service is rendered.

operating budget A projection of income and expense for the operation of a property over a one-year period.

operating costs A calculation of yearly costs of operation based on operating expenses from comparable properties and the maintenance needs of the subject property; used in preparing an annual operating budget.

optimum rents The ideal rent for a specific type of unit in a defined market area that may need to be adjusted to reflect specific advantages and disadvantages of the subject property.

percentage fees A property management fee expressed as a percentage of the gross collectible income from a property.

percentage lease A common retail lease requiring the tenant to pay a percentage of its gross income as rental consideration.

principal (1) An individual who designates another as his or her agent. (2) The original amount of a loan.

property analysis An analysis that familiarizes the manager with the nature and condition of a particular building and with its position relative to similar properties in the neighborhood.

proprietary lease The right of a member of a cooperative to occupy a unit in the building subject to certain conditions.

protected classes Any group of people that can be identified by a characteristic designated as such by the U.S. Department of Housing and Urban Development (HUD) in consideration of federal and state civil rights legislation. States may add groups for protection but may not delete any group designated by the federal laws.

radon A naturally occurring, odorless, colorless, radioactive gas that is a known carcinogen and has been found in every state and territory.

real property The earth's surface extending downward to the center and upward into space, including all things permanently attached thereto, by nature or by human hands.

recession Part of economic cycle in which growth slows.

research and development centers Provides assistance to facilities engineers and scientists at research universities, can assist with product marketing, and may provide incubator space for start-up companies.

reserve funds An expense category in the operating budget, monies, are set aside for replacement expenditures not covered by insurance, such as roof or furnace repairs.

residential property The type of property where people live. It includes privately owned dwellings as well as government and institutional ownership, and provides the greatest demand for professional property management.

resident manager A manager who resides at the managed property who coordinates and executes maintenance operations for the building and, in some cases, interfaces regularly with tenants.

retail property Commercial property from which goods are sold.

revival Part of economic cycle in which expansion begins again.

risk management That portion of property management that deals with minimizing or allocating risk of damage, such as utilizing insurance policies to transfer the risk of loss to a third party.

scattered-site rentals Rentals that are located in various parts of a city.

security deposit A payment by a tenant, held by the landlord during the lease term and kept (wholly or partially) on default or destruction of the premises by the tenant. Individual states set forth rules for holding, retaining, or returning security deposits.

special agent An agent who is only authorized to represent the principal on a specific matter or transaction, and once that transaction is concluded, the agency is terminated. A special agent has no authority to sign any contracts on behalf of the principal.

special-purpose property Hotels, resorts, nursing homes, theaters, schools, places of worship, and other businesses or organizations whose specialized needs dictate the design and operation of the building.

statute of frauds That part of state law that requires certain instruments, such as deeds, real estate contracts, and certain leases, to be in writing to be legally enforceable.

steering The directing of members of protected classes to buildings or neighborhoods that are already occupied primarily by members of those same classes and away from buildings and neighborhoods occupied primarily by members of other classes.

step-up clause A lease clause providing for rental rate increases of a definite amount at specific times over the term of the lease.

subletting Partial transfer of a tenant's right in a rental property to a third party.

supply and demand Economic principle that when the supply of a product is less than the demand for it, its price will increase; and when the supply of a product is greater than the demand, its price will decrease.

tenancy at sufferance A rental situation in which a tenant who originally obtained possession of the premises legally continues to occupy the property after the expiration of the leasehold interest and without the consent of the owner.

tenancy at will An estate that gives the tenant the right of possession for an indefinite period until the estate is terminated by either party or by the death of either party.

tenant emergency procedures manual Printed booklet outlining emergency organization, workday procedures, telephone numbers, and after-hours procedures during an emergency.

tenant wardens Employees of tenant companies who are schooled in emergency procedures by the building staff to direct their fellow employees during routine drills and actual emergencies.

testers People used to gather evidence for fair housing complaints.

triplexes Three-apartment building.

■ Chapter 1

Case Study Review

1. **c.** The federal Americans with Disabilities Act (ADA) is most applicable to commercial properties, including retail and office spaces. The ADA requires that public accommodations be readily accessible by anyone without regard to disability; that is, anyone with a physical or mental impairment that substantially limits one or more of his or her major life activities.

2. **d.** Typically, asset management in the real estate context refers to financial management of a sizable number of investment properties, and these managers often deal-supervise and are responsible for a portfolio of properties, rather than manage a single property, and will likely monitor financial performance, study local markets, and compare individual properties against a norm.

Review Questions

True-False

1. **TRUE.** A property manager's three main responsibilities are to generate income on behalf of the owners, achieve the owner's objectives, and preserve the property's value.

2. **FALSE.** The Institute of Real Estate Management (IREM) grants qualified management firms the designation of Accredited Management Organization (AMO®).

3. **FALSE.** Commercial real estate includes various types of income-producing properties, such as office buildings, shopping centers, stores, gas stations, and parking lots.

4. **FALSE.** According to the Census Bureau, more than 60 percent of U.S. housing is owner occupied.

5. **FALSE.** The federal Americans with Disabilities Act is most applicable to commercial properties, while fair housing laws protect accessibility to housing, either sales or rental.

6. **FALSE.** Retirement homes are examples of housing for the elderly. Nursing homes and hospitals are examples of special-use properties.

7. **TRUE.** Discrimination in housing on the basis of race, color, religion, national origin, sex, disability, and familial status is prohibited by federal, state, and local fair housing laws.

8. **TRUE.** The owner who takes money from the property and does not make any needed repairs is said to be milking the property, and property managers should avoid working with such individuals.

9. **TRUE.** A commercial property is generally considered to be a "public accommodation" and thus must meet accessibility requirements of the Americans with Disabilities Act.

10. **TRUE.** Real estate license laws vary greatly between states about who needs to be licensed before managing properties. There are vast differences between states as to who really needs a license, and if so, what kind.

Multiple-Choice

1. **b.** The property manager should attempt to generate the greatest possible net income for the owners of an investment property over that property's useful life.
2. **a.** The property manager's job is far more demanding than simply showing available space, executing leases, and collecting rents. The manager must have knowledge, communication skills, and technical expertise needed to be dynamic decision makers.
3. **d.** Rising land and construction costs have stimulated the growth of multi-family housing, because the economy of design and land usage inherent in multifamily housing allows for a lower per-family cost of construction.
4. **a.** Residential property is the largest source of demand for the services of professional property managers.
5. **d.** Federal fair housing laws prohibit discrimination in housing on the basis of race, color, religion, national origin, sex, disability, and familial status. When applying for a loan, discrimination is prohibited on the basis of age and/or marital status. Some cities and states do prohibit on the basis of sexual preference, but federal statutes do not.
6. **c.** Civil penalties include fines ranging from $11,000 for the first offense to more than $55,000 for multiple offenses within a seven-year period, in addition to awarding actual and punitive (unlimited) damages to the aggrieved parties. Penalties do not include imprisonment.
7. **d.** Commercial real estate includes various types of income-producing properties, such as office buildings, shopping centers, stores, gas stations, and parking lots. It does not include farms or mines.
8. **c.** The ADA requires managers to ensure that people with disabilities have full and equal access to facilities and services offered by any public accommodation; a commercial property is generally considered to be a "public accommodation"—a private entity that provides goods, services, facilities, or accommodations to the public.
9. **d.** Retail property includes freestanding buildings, traditional shopping centers, malls, and specialized centers—places where goods are sold.
10. **b.** The traditional separation between office space and manufacturing or warehouse facilities is breaking down in many business and industrial parks, which now offer combinations of office and industrial space or buildings that are divided into differently sized units for use by growing companies.
11. **c.** Because property for heavy industry must be designed with the specific needs of potential users in mind, such plants are generally occupied and managed by the owner.
12. **d.** Ministorage facilities offer extra storage space to homeowners, apartment dwellers, and businesses. Concierge services provide business services, small equipment rentals and personal services to tenants.
13. **b.** The manager should identify and analyze the owner's goals, which will vary widely among the individual, corporate, fiduciary, and government owners.

14. **b.** In 1933, a group of property management firms created the Institute of Real Estate Management (IREM), which is today an affiliate group of the National Association of REALTORS® (NAR).

15. **c.** The Registered Apartment Manager (RAM) certification is the oldest residential property management certification program in the United States. The certification is also approved by the Department of Housing and Urban Development (HUD) as providing quality training to managers of multifamily rental, condominium, cooperative, subsidized, and market-rate housing.

■ Chapter 2

Case Study Review

1. **a.** Having learned from his previous experience, Doug can try to devote the large part of his time to maintaining sound owner relations by sending a personal letter with each monthly report or possibly having lunch with the client from time to time.

2. **b.** A transitional team can develop expertise to ensure a smooth acquisition for every new property. Doug will always need to be marketing and working to maintain good relationships with his owners.

Review Questions

True-False

1. **TRUE.** Usually, the property manager is a general agent of the owner empowered to make decisions in a variety of situations.

2. **FALSE.** The agent is responsible to obey lawful instructions; if the owner suggests any illegal activity, the manager should resign from the agreement.

3. **FALSE.** The manager should never commingle client funds with company funds. Client funds should be deposited in a trust account.

4. **FALSE.** The percentage fee is a wonderful incentive for the manager who needs to improve the income of the building, although a minimum fee may be established to protect management fees if the building revenue drops.

5. **TRUE.** A manager's legal and professional responsibility and liability as a fiduciary are the same regardless of the amount of compensation. In fact, a gratuitous agent (one who works for no fee at all) may be held liable for negligence in failing to perform a duty.

6. **FALSE.** The fee structure must be negotiated between the owner and the manager, and must be set independently. Fees must not be discussed with other, competing property management firms. No trade association determines fees.

7. **TRUE.** The owner is responsible for providing the manager or management agency with all data necessary for the efficient operation of the property.

8. **TRUE.** The manager should personally inspect the property as part of the takeover.

9. **TRUE.** Tenant security deposit balances and accounting are an essential part of any takeover. In many states, failure to return deposits or pay interest when required is a violation of the landlord-tenant law and is

grounds for real estate licensee disciplinary action, in addition to costly monetary damages.

10. **TRUE.** The manager must know what kind and frequency of communication the owner wants, and the types of information that are important to which owners, and must make sure that the owners are informed accordingly.

Multiple-Choice

1. **b.** An agent has a fiduciary relationship to his or her principal, which is a confidential relationship marked by trust and confidence that requires the highest degree of loyalty on the part of the agent. The agent must always put the property owner's interests first, above his or her own interests.

2. **a.** The written contract creating the agency relationship is called the management contract; it empowers the property manager, as agent, to act on behalf of the owner, or principal, in certain situations.

3. **b.** In lieu of a formalized contract between employer and employee, a written authorization to sign leases should be given to the employee. This authorization is sometimes limited in the dollar amount or length of lease.

4. **d.** A general agent can act on behalf of the principal on a range of matters and can obligate the principal to any contracts signed by the agent that are within the scope of that agent's duties. A special agent has no authority to sign any contracts on behalf of the principal.

5. **c.** An agent, whether specific or general, has certain duties that are imposed by agency law, specifically a fiduciary relationship, which is a confidential relationship marked by trust and confidence that requires the highest degree of loyalty on the part of the agent.

6. **c.** An agent may terminate early when the owner causes the agent damages or liability, but termination by the agent due to an owner's illegal acts does not release the owner from his or her obligations under the contract terms.

7. **d.** As common practice, the agent should not advance his or her own funds to cover a deficiency. The amount of the reserve fund should be proportional to the size of the property.

8. **b.** Most state laws virtually always prohibit commingling by the property manager. Commingling involves combining the owner's funds with the property manager's business or personal funds.

9. **d.** The fee structure must be negotiated between the owner and the manager and must be set independently. Fees must not be discussed with other, competing property management firms.

10. **c.** The percentage fee is a wonderful incentive for the manager who needs to improve the income of the building, although a minimum fee may be established to protect management fees if the building revenue drops.

11. **d.** To ensure a smooth takeover of a property, the owner should provide all necessary documents, and the manager should use a takeover checklist and personally inspect the entire property. No one should offer the tenants an opportunity to terminate their leases.

12. **c.** In many states, failure to return deposits or pay interest when required is a violation of the landlord-tenant law and is grounds for real estate licensee disciplinary action, in addition to costly monetary damages.

13. **b.** The principal means of regular communication between the manager and the owner or owning corporation is the monthly earnings report,

and the manager should include a personal note along with the financial information.

14. **b.** A flat-fee arrangement is most appropriate when managing condominiums. These owners want management to contain expenses, not increase them.

15. **b.** Any information that may pertain to the fiscal affairs of the property, such as serving an eviction notice, should be noted to the owner monthly.

■ Chapter 3

Case Study Review

1. **c.** Charles should note that commercial tenants are shifting to lower-priced properties whenever they can. His investor may wish to buy more residential rental properties and may have to reduce rents to retain current commercial tenants.

2. **b.** Often, when a factory closes, its workers are thrown out of work and lose their incomes. Many cannot afford their mortgage payments, and housing values decrease, but the residential rental market often increases. This may be an opportunity for Charles's investor.

Review Questions

True-False

1. **FALSE.** Seasonal variations occur at regular intervals either because of custom or nature. Construction slows in cold winter months; college students rent in the fall.

2. **TRUE.** A business cycle consists of four phases: expansion, recession, contraction, and revival.

3. **TRUE.** Long-term economic movements are usually measured over terms of at least 50 years and reflect the overall direction the economy is taking.

4. **FALSE.** To assist the owner, the property manager must first understand basic economic trends and their implications for the real estate market. With this information, the property manager can assess the current and future potential of a property in order to develop a management plan for it.

5. **FALSE.** The most important element of a management plan is an analysis of the owner's objectives, in addition to a regional and neighborhood analysis and a specific property analysis.

6. **FALSE.** Knowledge of zoning ordinances and building codes is useful to the property manager when performing a neighborhood analysis, since these could restrict the neighborhood's growth.

7. **TRUE.** When taking over a new property, the manager should begin with a careful study of each tenant's lease to learn the amount and durability of rental income. To avoid surprises, the manager should be alert for concessions, renewal options, and termination notices.

8. **FALSE.** The building's exterior appearance greatly influences the tenant's initial impressions of the property and can affect its desirability.

9. **FALSE.** The antitrust provisions prevent competitors from discussing and fixing prices. Many managers do rely on regional norms that are available through trade associations, trade journals, and professional real estate management organizations.

10. **TRUE.** Ultimately, the owner's objectives will be the deciding factor in the adoption of the management plan.

Multiple-Choice

1. **d**. A market is defined as an exchange of goods and services between willing sellers and willing buyers. There is no single real estate market; rather, the real estate market is made up of the scattered, unrelated transactions that occur between property buyers and sellers and landlords and tenants.

2. **c**. A business cycle consists of four phases: expansion, when production increases; recession, when supply meets and begins to surpass demand; contraction, when fewer products are made; and revival, when consumers begin to venture back into the market.

3. **c**. Hurricane Katrina certainly fits the description of random changes since no one ever expected so much damage, including major population shifts experienced after Katrina. Winter storms and nine-month college schedules are more predictable and can be planned for. Outsourcing of jobs is a long-term movement, and no one quite knows how that will ultimately affect the economy.

4. **a**. Indirect government actions, such as reducing taxes and/or introducing affordable housing programs, also have significant impact on business cycles.

5. **a**. Specific cycles in the residential rental market correspond roughly to cycles in multifamily residential housing starts.

6. **c**. The basic blueprint of a property manager's responsibilities is the management plan, the financial and operational strategy for the ongoing management of a property.

7. **d**. The manager draws up the management plan and budget on the basis of regional and neighborhood market analysis, analysis of the subject property itself, and an analysis of the owner's objectives for the property. The operating budget is only a small part of the overall plan.

8. **b**. Reserve funds cover the "unexpected expenditures that may be expected." Any budget forecast, whether an operating budget or a five-year projection, should provide for reserve funds under the expense category.

9. **c**. Gross rental income is determined by multiplying the amount of space in the building by the base rental rate for that type of space. Anticipated income is the amount after deducting rent loss and adding in other income.

10. **b**. Cash flow is the amount of money available for use after paying expenses and the debt service (the mortgage), and is determined by subtracting the total adjusted operating costs plus debt service from the anticipated revenue for the coming year.

11. **c**. The first step in formulating any financial planning reports is establishing optimum rents for that particular property. Optimum rents are the ideal rent for a specific type of unit in a defined market area that may need to be adjusted to reflect specific advantages and disadvantages of the subject property.

12. **d**. The objective in a market analysis is to arrive at the optimum price for a standard unit of that type within the market area. From this figure, the expected base income for the property can be calculated.

13. **d**. The terms of the lease will disclose the amount and durability of rental income.

14. **b.** Prospective tenants form their initial impressions of the premises based on what they see as they approach the building, the "curb appeal."
15. **b.** Although the property and neighborhood analyses and five-year forecast are important, the owner's objectives will ultimately determine the acceptance or rejection of the management plan.

■ Chapter 4

Case Study Review

1. **c.** Chin should consider revising future lease documents to include a provision for a late penalty that would encourage tenants to pay the rent on time.
2. **c.** At the very least, Chin should meet with Juarez to gain insight into problems with the complex or problems with Chin's management style. Even if Chin loses Juarez as a tenant, she may learn something to head off any kind of "revolt" fostered by Samuels.

Review Questions

True-False

1. **FALSE.** Although many property managers are responsible for leasing, property managers dealing with cooperatives and condominium communities are not responsible for leasing the owner-occupied units.
2. **FALSE.** Very few leaseholds are estates at will, which are usually oral with no definite beginning or ending dates.
3. **TRUE.** A holdover tenancy is created when the tenant holding an estate for years remains in possession of the premises after the expiration of the lease. Acceptance of rental payments by the owner or property manager is considered legal proof of the owner's acquiescence to the holdover tenancy.
4. **TRUE.** Tenancy at sufferance occurs when a tenant obtains possession of the premises legally but then remains on the property without the owner's consent after the leasehold interest has expired. This tenant has no right to possession.
5. **TRUE.** Under a gross lease, sometimes called a straight lease, the tenant pays a fixed rental amount and the owner pays all other expenses for the property.
6. **FALSE.** The percentage lease is commonly used for retail property, especially malls. It usually provides for the payment of a fixed base rental fee plus a percentage of the tenant's gross income in excess of a predetermined minimum amount of sales.
7. **TRUE.** Written, oral, and implied leases are all covered by the statute of frauds in the state in which the property is located.
8. **TRUE.** The contract is a lease; the consideration is the promise to pay rent.
9. **FALSE.** Subletting transfers only part of the interest. Assignment of a lease transfers all of the tenant's remaining right in the property to a third party. Note that neither relieves the original tenant for being responsible for the rental payments.
10. **FALSE.** In a few circumstances, if the modifications are too costly or extremely difficult to make, an exemption may be granted. However, no one should assume that an exemption will be granted.

Multiple-Choice

1. **d.** The foundation for good landlord-tenant relations begins with a clearly written lease, clear understanding of the rules and regulations, and the establishment of a good communication system with tenants.
2. **b.** At the beginning of the tenancy, the manager should inspect the premises with the tenant to determine if promised repairs or alterations have been made or are in progress. Both the manager and the tenant should sign the form, each should keep a copy, and the same form should be used at the time the tenant leaves.
3. **c.** Whenever a service request is made, the tenant should be told immediately when it will be taken care of or told that it will not be done.
4. **b.** A stable tenant with a record of timely rental payments is a proven quantity and an asset to the owner, because the present tenant will probably make fewer demands for redecorating or other alterations than a new occupant would, representing an additional savings.
5. **b.** From the outset, the manager should be clear as to when rent is due, where it is to be paid, and the penalties for being late or not making a payment.
6. **a.** Under no circumstances should the manager be involved in any discussion of any fair housing protected classes.
7. **d.** Notice of the new rates should be given to the tenants more than 30 days before the lease renewal and possibly as much as three to six months in advance. It is advisable to explain, if possible, the reason for the higher rates, which could possibly include upgrades, major repairs, more amenities, and more service.
8. **b.** Constructive eviction occurs when the tenant must actually abandon the premises due to the owner's negligence in supplying essential services, such as failing to supply heat or water.
9. **c.** From the outset, the manager should be clear as to when rent is due, where it is to be paid, and the penalties for being late or not making payments.
10. **d.** When a security deposit is refunded to a tenant, it should be accompanied by another letter explaining any deductions from the deposit. (In fact, this is usually required by law.)
11. **c.** It is advisable to explain, if possible, the reason for the higher rates, which could possibly include upgrades, major repairs, more amenities, and more service.
12. **d.** There should be a predetermined, fixed, reasonable period of time between the due date and the announcement of legal action for delinquency that in most cases should not exceed three to five days.
13. **c.** The postoccupancy inspection should be conducted with the tenant after the tenant has removed all personal items.
14. **d.** The manager should use the same move-in form for the move-out to determine if any damage has been done to the property and if the unit is in reasonable condition.
15. **b.** Generally, in most states, the property manager must provide the tenant with a written statement of deductions; failure to follow this procedure can result in severe criminal and civil penalties.

■ Chapter 5

Case Study Review

1. **b.** Han's complaint is a serious one, and Harriet should respond accordingly. She should personally see that the repair is made in a timely fashion. She should make a note of Han's complaint and record the actions that she takes to look into and correct the situation. She should examine all of the records to see if there is any evidence of a discriminatory pattern.

2. **c.** Harriet should examine her office policies to make sure they comply with fair housing rules and emphasize her office's commitment to non-discriminatory practices. She should discuss the issue regularly at office meetings and select someone to be a compliance officer to help keep everyone in the office up-to-date.

Review Questions

True-False

1. **FALSE.** While specific application of the property management techniques may have to be modified to the circumstance, the basic principles here have universal application, whether to scattered-site housing, apartment buildings, or condominium and cooperative housing.

2. **TRUE.** Scattered-site rentals are often located in various parts of a city. Properly maintaining and showing properties to prospective tenants may involve unproductive travel to and from various locations.

3. **FALSE.** In cooperative ownership, the apartment owner purchases shares in the corporation (or partnership or trust) that holds title to the entire apartment building. The ownership of the building can be either trust or corporate in nature.

4. **FALSE.** Each condominium unit is a statutory entity that may be mortgaged, taxed, sold, or otherwise transferred in ownership, independently of all other units in the condo project.

5. **TRUE.** Because the condo owners' association governing board is an elected body that changes frequently, the manager should negotiate a contract for a guaranteed and reasonably long term. Otherwise, the manager may never receive adequate compensation for the time and effort expended in managing the property.

6. **TRUE.** Federal fair housing laws (as well as state and city fair housing laws) are designed to guarantee everyone an equal opportunity to live wherever they can afford and choose to live.

7. **FALSE.** Historically, managers were steering when they put the white tenants in one building or on one floor, and all of the Asian Americans, African Americans, or any nonwhites in another building or floor. A more current example of steering is congregating all families with children in one building or on one floor away from tenants without children.

8. **TRUE.** To calculate net operating income, subtract the total expenses from the total annual anticipated income.

9. **FALSE.** It is unwise to increase present cash flow by deferring expenditures for real maintenance needs, thus upsetting existing tenants. It is better to generate savings through volume buying or through an energy conservation program.

10. **TRUE.** An owner's pro rata share for each unit is determined by state statute and/or the ratio the square footage of the unit bears to the total square footage of all units in the project. It is expressed as a percentage, such as 1.034 percent.

Multiple-Choice

1. **b.** The principal difference between managing single-family homes and managing apartments centers on geography and time because scattered-site rentals are often located in various parts of a city.

2. **c.** Market surveys of comparable residential properties and economic conditions in the immediate area are absolutely essential in gauging any property's viability as an income-producing investment and in establishing a rental schedule for the apartments.

3. **b.** Duplexes and triplexes with common areas including front, side, and backyards require harmonious cooperation among occupants. Thus, the tenants must be compatible, a condition not usually as strong a factor when renting in larger communities.

4. **a.** The property manager of a cooperative or a condominium works for a group of owner-occupants and, therefore, has no responsibility for maintaining occupancy levels.

5. **a.** A cooperative or condominium management is concerned primarily with maintaining the integrity of the premises and achieving the mutual goals of the owner/occupants.

6. **c.** Financial reports for cooperatives and condominiums are basically modified versions of those used for apartment buildings.

7. **b.** Condominium and cooperative management fees are usually a flat fee that has been calculated using a cost-per-unit method or the management pricing worksheet.

8. **d.** The manager's decision to hire full-time or contract services must be based on the amount of services required and the cost-effectiveness to the owner.

9. **a.** The manager should not be involved in selling any product to the tenants. The manager should be aware of any possible sources of income. In addition to the rents, parking and storage fees and vending and laundry machines can provide additional income.

10. **d.** The after-tax cash flow analysis allows the owner to analyze actual return on investment after taxes and decide whether it is economically more advantageous to keep the property, invest more money in it, refinance it, or sell it.

11. **a.** Steering may also occur when the manager tells the prospect that there is no vacancy, when, in fact, there is a vacancy. This misstatement, which is illegal when it is made on the basis of any of the protected classes, steers the prospect away from the manager's building.

12. **d.** In a court action, however, a judge or jury can award unlimited punitive damages to the aggrieved party. Also, the prevailing party may be awarded reasonable attorney's fees and costs.

13. **c.** The manager should definitely *not* make tenant selection based on the applicant's race or religion. The manager should make sure that tenant selection is objective, relevant to fulfilling lease obligations, and applied equally to every applicant.

14. **b.** The resident manager is one of the most important people on the management team, as he or she may be the only person the tenant ever meets. Consequently, the resident manager must possess a variety of

skills: able to manage tenants and maintenance personnel, adept at accounting for money and supplies, and aware of community issues and tenant concerns, all the while balancing the owner's wishes with the tenant's demands.

15. **a.** Although cash flow projections appear to be complex, they deal only with previously used data to show the effect that the investment property has on the owner's income in terms of tax benefits.

■ Chapter 6

Case Study Review

1. **d.** Susan should immediately hire a security firm, which will demonstrate to her tenants that she is aware of their immediate safety concerns. She should contact her insurance agent to review flood coverage and should have the insurance agent contact the tenants to discuss renters' insurance. Unfortunately, if the crime occurs after hours, a watch organized by the tenants may not be too helpful.

2. **c.** Kim should draw up procedures to follow in the event of any major type of emergency, including flooding. She cannot sell insurance to her tenants. She should walk the property to determine if any improvements can be made to discourage crime; for example, she might change the landscaping and install more lighting in the parking lot.

Review Questions

True-False

1. **FALSE.** Building security no longer simply means the presence of a night watchman. Security is a 24/7 responsibility, and the modern approach to dealing with emergencies such as fire and natural disasters focuses on prevention and safety.

2. **TRUE.** A good life safety and security program is based on four goals: prevention, detection, containment, and counteraction.

3. **FALSE.** The owner can only buy insurance on property that the owner owns. Each tenant is responsible for insuring his or her own personal property.

4. **FALSE.** Mold does not require light in order to grow. It does require a cellulosic food source and moisture. Property managers should do as much as possible to contain excess moisture.

5. **FALSE.** The first priority of any safety and security program is the preservation of human life.

6. **TRUE.** From a legal standpoint, official emergency crews are in control as soon as they enter the building.

7. **TRUE.** Flood insurance policies must be purchased separately, and subsidized policies are available to any property owner located in a community participating in the National Flood Insurance Program (NFIP).

8. **FALSE.** During an emergency, the property manager should cooperate fully with media, authorities, and other segments of the public. Admissions of liability or speculations about the cause of an accident or damage to property of others should be avoided, and no estimates of the extent of the damage or the amount of reconstruction costs should be made until they can be accurately assessed.

9. **TRUE.** The property manager should make a printed tenant emergency procedures manual available to tenants that includes procedures for many emergency situations.
10. **TRUE.** Buying insurance is an owner's method of transferring risk to the insurers or to third parties.

Multiple-Choice

1. **d.** A good life safety and security program with loss reduction plans and emergency preparedness is an example of controlling the risk.
2. **c.** An example of transferring the risk is buying insurance.
3. **d.** Flood insurance may never be added to a building insurance policy, nor can an endorsement be added. Flood insurance policies must always be purchased separately.
4. **a.** Carbon monoxide is a result of incomplete burning of fossil fuels. It is a problem in any space without adequate ventilation.
5. **d.** Asbestos management and control was an important concern for commercial property managers in the 1990s but is lessening today.
6. **b.** Managers of any residential property built before 1978, with a few exceptions, are required to notify tenants about possible lead-based paint and provide copies of the EPA lead-hazard information booklet, *Protecting Your Family from Lead in Your Home*.
7. **a.** Radon is an invisible, odorless, and tasteless radioactive gas that occurs naturally and has been linked to lung cancer. Carbon monoxide is also colorless, odorless, and tasteless, but it is a deadly poison that impacts nearly immediately.
8. **b.** The federal Lead-Based Paint Hazard Reductions Act (LBPHRA) requires that copies of the disclosures be retained for three years.
9. **b.** The manager should also carry errors and omissions insurance (with limits of at least 10 percent of the total annual collections) to protect against possible accounting mistakes or other oversights, including failure to act.
10. **d.** Generally, a good life safety and security program is a three-pronged approach that incorporates skilled use of equipment, personnel, and procedures.
11. **b.** The first priority of a life safety and security program is the protection of human life.
12. **c.** All communications should come from a designated person in the life safety control center. This person can be assisted by tenant wardens.
13. **d.** Some areas of a property are more susceptible to criminal activity and require extra care. Landscaping should not provide hiding places near cars or walkways; lighting should be improved to increase customer confidence the number of patrol vehicles should be increased; patrol vehicles can be made more visible with brightly colored markings; and customer service booths can be installed at strategic places in the parking lot.
14. **d.** In any building emergency—from a partially flooded floor due to a plumbing breakdown to a total conflagration—it is imperative that the property manager make immediate contact with each tenant.
15. **b.** Following a disaster, the property manager must concentrate on preventing further damage and on minimizing loss.

A

Abandoned property, 53
Accessibility, fair housing laws and, 71–72
Accounting, 17
Accredited Management Organization (AMO®), 9
Actual damages, 72
Actual eviction, 55
Adjustable-rate mortgages (ARMs), 32
Advertising
    discriminatory, 68, 80
    equal housing opportunity classified ads, 71
Agency responsibilities
    fiduciary, 16–18
    scope of agency authority, 16
Agent, 16
Air-conditioning, and chlorofluorocarbons (CFCs), 87–88
Alterations to property, by tenant, 52
Americans with Disabilities Act (ADA), 4, 52, 71
Antitrust laws, 4, 23
Apartment building
    case study, 78
    maintenance, 73
    operating reports, 73–76
    resident manager's responsibilities, 73
ARMs (adjustable-rate mortgages), 32
Asbestos, 87
Asset management services, 7
Assignment of lease, 52

B

Background checks, 5
Bankruptcy default clauses, 56
Base of operations, 90
Blockbusting, 68
Building codes and regulations, 34
Building Owners and Managers Association International (BOMA), 9
Building Owners and Managers Institute, 9
Building rules, 51
Building systems, 89–90
Business cycles, 30–31, 42
Business economy
    cyclic fluctuations, 30–31
    government influences on, 31
    long-term movements, 31

random changes, 31
    seasonal variations, 30
Business parks, 6

C

Capital expenditures, 39, 77
Carbon monoxide, 87
Cash flow
    analysis, after improvement *vs.* ROI in "as is" condition, 39
    analysis, after-tax, 75–76, 80
    owner objectives and, 37
    reports, 77
Casualty damage, 52
Central base of operations, 90
Certified Property Manager (CPM) designation, 9
Certified Shopping Center Manager, 10
Chattel fixtures, 52
Children
    housing discrimination and, 69
    residential leases and, 51
Chlorofluorocarbons (CFCs), 87–88
Civil Rights Act of 1866, 68, 80
Civil Rights Act of 1968 Title VII (Fair Housing Act), 4. *See also* Fair Housing Act
Commercial property (commercial real estate), 11
    categories, 5–6
    rental market, 32
    trade or chattel fixtures installed by tenants, 52–53
Commingling of funds, 17
Common elements, 77
Communication
    owner-manager, 24–25
    with tenants, 92
Comparable properties, 36–37
Comparative income and expense analysis, 41
Compliance clause, in lease, 52
Concierge services, 7
Condominiums, 66–67, 80
    covenants, conditions, and restrictions (CC&Rs), 67
    expenses, 77
    governing boards of, 67
    legal structures of, 66
    management fees, 78
    operating reports, 77
    pro rata share, calculating, 77

Constructive eviction, 55
Consumer price index, 51
Continuing education, 4
Contraction phase, 30
Contract (management agreement), 16–17, 18–19
Convalescent care facilities, 3
Cooperatives, 66–67, 80
    legal structures of, 66
    management fees, 78
    operating reports, 77
Corporate property managers, 7
Cost-of-living index, 51
Costs, reducing, 76
Covenants, conditions, and restrictions (CC&Rs), 67
Criminal activity issues, 94–95
Criminal background checks, 5
Curb appeal, 36

D

Damage
    insurance policies and, 93
    minimizing post-emergency, 93–94
Demographics, 32
Descriptions (legal description of property), 49
Disabled tenants
    anticipating needs of, 89
    fair housing and, 69–70
Disaster aftershocks, 93–94
Disbursements, 18
Disclosure, 18, 53
Discrimination, 4
    fair housing laws and, 68–72
    proprietary leases and, 67
    protected classes, 68
Duplexes, 65

E

Earnings statements, 18
Economics and planning
    business cycles, 30–31
    case study, 41
    general business economy, 30–31
    management plan, 33, 37–41
    market analysis, 33–35
    owner objectives, analysis of, 37
    property analysis, 35–37
    real estate economy, 32–33
    recognizing trends, 33

"Elderly" classification, 3
Electronic equipment, 89
Elevators, 89, 93
Emergencies
    emergency equipment and
      technologies, 89, 91
    emergency procedures guide,
      92, 96
    emergency spokesperson, 91
    media coverage of, 93
Employee crime, 95
Environmental issues, management of,
    87–88, 96
Equal Credit Opportunity Act (ECOA), 5
Equal housing poster, 69, 70
Equilibrium, 30
Equipment, analysis of, 36
Errors and omissions insurance, 86
Escalation clause, 51
Escalation leases, 50
Essential services, failure to supply, 55
Estate for years, 47
Estate from period to period, 47
Evacuation drills, 91
Eviction
    actual removal, 59
    proceedings, 55
    terminating the tenancy in court,
      59
Expansion phase, 30
Exterior appearance, of property, 36

F
Failure to act, 86
Fair Housing Act, 4. *See also* Ameri-
    cans with Disabilities Act (ADA)
    avoiding violations, 72
    blockbusting, 69
    compliance, 65
    disabled tenants and, 70–71
    discriminatory advertising, 68
    enforcement, 71–72
    equal housing poster, 69, 70
    familial status, 4, 69–70
    steering, 69
    testers, 71
Familial status, and fair housing, 4,
    69–70
"Fetch" dogs, 71
Fiduciary duties, 16
Financing, discrimination prohibited
    in, 5
Fire
    damage, 52
    detection, 91
Five-year forecast, 39, 40, 42
Flood insurance, 86
Forcible entry and detainer suit, 55
Freon™, 87

G
General agent, 16, 17
Government influences, on economy, 31
Graduated leases, 50
Gross collectible rental income, 37–38
Gross lease, 48
Gross scheduled rental income, 37
Guide dogs, 71

H
Hazard detection, 91
Hazard insurance, 86
Hazardous substances and waste, 87
Health hazards, 36
Heavy manufacturing, 6
Holdover tenancy, 47
Holt, George A., 9
Homes for the aged, 3
Housing starts, 32
HUD (Department of Housing and
    Urban Development), 10
    elderly or near elderly housing
      requirements, 69
    Fair Housing Information
      Clearinghouse, 71
    HUD Design Manual, 71
    manufactured housing
      specifications, 3

I
Improvements to property, by tenant,
    52
Incubator spaces, 6
Independent agent managers, 22
Independent living facilities, 3
Index lease, 50
Industrial property, 6–7
    industrial parks, 6
    trade or chattel fixtures installed
      by tenants, 52–53
Inspection procedures (safety), 92
Institute of Real Estate Management
    (IREM), 9
Insurable interest, 86
Insurance, 85–87
Interior space, determining, 36
Internal safety procedures, 91
International Council of Shopping
    Centers (ICSC), 10

J
Jones v. Alfred H. Mayer Company (1968),
    68, 80

L
Landlord-tenant relationship case
    study, 59
    knowledge of landlord-tenant
      laws, 46
    managing tenant relations, 56–59
    rights/obligations of landlords
      and tenants, 51–54
Laundry machines, 74
Lead-Based Paint Hazard Reduction
    Act (LBPHRA), 5, 88
Lead-based paint, 88
Lease(s)
    anticipation of changing circum-
      stances and, 50
    basic lease forms, 48–49
    details of, 46
    essential provisions of, 49–56
    formats, 56
    manager authority to sign, 15
    minimizing liability for criminal
      activity, 95
    in property analysis, 35–36
    purpose of, 45
    renewals, 50, 57
    signing of, 49
    terminating the tenancy, 58
    terminating the tenancy in court,
      59
    understanding of terms, 57
    use of premises, 51
Leasehold estates, 46–48
    estate for years, 47
    estate from period to period, 47
    tenancy at sufferance, 48
    tenancy at will, 47
Leasing agent, 8
Leasing fees, 23
Licensing laws, 8, 11
Life safety and security. *See* Safety Life
    safety officers, 88–89
Light manufacturing, 6
Limited common elements, 77
Locations, potential hazardous, 94
Loft buildings, 7
Long-term movements (of economy), 31
Loss rates, 36–37
Loyalty, 16

M
Maintenance of premises
    handling requests for, 57, 58
    owner obligations for, 54
    personnel, 73
    resident manager's responsibili-
      ties for, 73
    specified in contract, 22
Management agreement (contract)
    agent authority listed in, 21
    authority for employee hiring/
      supervision/firing, etc., 22
    purpose of, 45
Management fees, condos and co-ops,
    78

Management plan, 33, 37–41
  comparative income and expense analysis, 39
  five-year forecast, 39, 40, 42
  operating budget, 38, 42
  presentation, 39
Management pricing worksheet, 78, 79
Manager-owner relationship, 14–25
  agency responsibilities, 16–18
  case study, 25–26
  contract period, 18
  employer-employee relationship, 15, 26
  formal fiduciary, or trust, relationship, 15
  identification of parties/property, 18
  management fees of independent agents, 22–23
  owner's responsibilities, 21–22
  personal and ongoing contact, 25
  principal-agent relationship, 15–16, 26
  property manager's responsibilities, 18–21
  takeover procedures, 23–26
  trustor-trustee relationship, 15, 26
Manufactured home parks, 3
Manufacturing, 6
Market, defined, 30
Market analysis, 33–35
  data evaluation, 35
  neighborhood, 34–35
  regional, 34
Market trends, 39
Media coverage, of emergencies, 93
Megan's law, 5
"Milking a property", 9
Ministorage facilities, 7
Mold, 87
Monthly reports, 18, 24–25
Move-in inspections, 56
Multifamily properties, 3, 65–66

N

Name of Parties (specified in lease), 49
National Apartment Association (NAA), 10
National Association of REALTORS® (NAR), 9
National Association of Residential Property Managers, 10
National Flood Insurance Program, 86
National Multi Housing Council, 10
"Near elderly" classification, 3
Neighborhood
  amenities and facilities, 35
  boundaries, 34

economy, 34
market analysis, 34–35
Net lease, 48

O

Obedience, 17
Occupancy of the premises (specified in lease), 50
Occupancy rates, 35
Office property, 6
Operating budget, 38, 42, 74
Operating reports (apartment), 73–76
  additional income, 74–75
  after-tax cash flow analysis, 75–76
  operating budgets, 74
Operating reports (condos and co-ops), 77
Optimum rent, 35, 37
Oral lease agreement, 49
Owner breach, 18
Owner objectives, 9. *See also* Manager-owner relationship
  analysis of, 37
  cash flow considerations, 38
  comparative income and expense analysis and, 41
Owner's responsibilities, 21–22

P

Panic selling, 69
Parking fees, 74
Partial eviction, 55
Passthrough, 51
Percentage fees, 22
Percentage lease, 48–49
Periodic lease, 47
Personnel
  assignments, 90–91
  employee crime, 95
  maintenance, 73
  role of, in property management, 90
Physical inventory, of space, 36–37
Police department, 91
Population trends, 32
Possession of premises
  failure to deliver, 54
  specified in lease, 50
Profitability, gauging, 72–73
Property analysis, 35–37
  comparables, 36–37
  physical condition, 36
Property description, 49
Property inspection, 36–37
Property management/manager. *See also* Manager-owner relationship
  areas of competency necessary for, 8
  building systems, 89–90

case study, 10, 95
communication with tenants and, 92
continuing education for, 4
criminal activity issues, 94–95
disclosing name/address of, 53
duties and responsibilities of, 7–11, 18–21
emergency equipment and technologies, 89
emergency preparedness procedures, 92
employee crime and, 95
environmental issues, 87–88
knowledge of landlord-tenant laws, 46
liability and, 23
licensing laws, 11
life safety officers, 88–89
management agreement, 19–20
minimizing post-emergency damage, 93
personnel assignments, 90–91
professional organizations/ designations, 9
property management procedures, 91–93
property manager defined, 2
regulation and licensing requirements for, 66
right to enter/inspect premises, 54
safety procedures and, 91–93
state licensing laws, 8
tenant emergency procedures manual, 93
Property owner. *See also* Manager-owner relationship
  maintenance and, 54
  objectives, 37
  obligations, 53–54
Proprietary lease, 66
Protected classes, 68
"Protecting Your Family from Lead in Your Home,", 88
Punitive damages, 72

Q

Quiet enjoyment covenant, 53

R

Radon, 87
Random changes (of economy), 30
Real estate economy, 32–33
Real property
  industrial property, 6–7
  residential, 2–5
  special-purpose property, 7
Real Property Administrator (RPA), 9

Reasonable care, 16
Recession phase, 30
Regional market analysis, 34
Rent
    adjustments (specified in lease),
      50–51
    collections, 57
    default, 56
    increases, management of, 57–58
    optimum rent, 35, 37
    security deposits and, 8
Rental agreement
    noncompliance by owner, 54–55
    noncompliance by tenant, 55–56
Rental market, 32
Rental schedule, 72
Renters' insurance, 52, 86
Repairs, specified in management
    contract, 22
Research and development centers, 6
Reserve funds, 38, 77
Residential Management Professional
    (RMP), 10
Residential properties (residential real
    estate), 2–5, 11, 64–81
    apartment buildings, 73–76
    case study, 78
    condominiums and cooperatives,
      66–67, 77–78
    facilities for the aging, 3
    management pricing worksheet, 79
    manufactured home parks, 3
    market analysis, 72–73
    multifamily, 3, 65–66
    overview, 64–65
    single-family homes, duplexes,
      and triplexes, 2–3, 65
    tenant relations and fair housing
      laws, 68–72
Residential rental market, 32
Restrictive clauses, 51
Retail property, 6, 48–49
Retirement communities, 3
Retrofitting, 89
Revival phase, 29

Rights and obligations (specified in
    lease), 51–52
Risk management, 85–87

S
Safety
    criminal activity issues, 94–95
    emergency preparedness, 92–93
    environmental issues, 87–88
    hazards, 36
    inspection procedures, 92
    managing life safety and security,
      88–91
    minimizing post-emergency
      damage, 93–94
    risk management, 85–87
    safety drills, 90
Scattered-site rentals, 65
Seasonal variations, in economy, 30
Security deposit(s), 8, 53
    returned to tenant, 57
    takeover procedures and, 24
Security personnel, 94
Sex offender registration, 5
Single-family homes, 2–3, 65
Smoke detectors, 90
Special agent, 16, 17
Special-purpose property, 7
Sprinkler systems, 90
Statute of frauds, 49
Steering, 69
Step-up clause, 50
Storage fees, 74
Straight lease (gross lease), 48
Structural inspections, 92
Subletting, 52
Suit for eviction, 55
Suit for possession, 55
Supply and demand principle, 30, 35

T
Taxes
    condominium owners and, 67
    cooperative expenses deduction,
      66

Technological expertise, 8
Telephones or telephone jacks, 89
Tenancy at sufferance, 48
Tenancy at will, 47
Tenancy for years, 47
Tenant(s)
    communication with, 92
    damages to unit by, 55
    illegal activities by, 56
    obligations, 52–53
    remedies for noncompliance of
      lease obligations, 54–55
Tenant emergency procedures manual,
    93
Tenant wardens, 91
Termination notice
    in estate for years, 47
    in tenancy at will, 47
Term of lease, 50
Testers (of discriminatory practices), 71
Total anticipated revenue, 37–38
Trade fixtures, 52–53
Transportation, 34–35
Triple-net lease, 48
Triplexes, 65
Trusts and trustees, 15

U
Uniform Residential Landlord and
    Tenant Act, 53
Unit ownership declaration, 77
Use of premises (specified in lease), 51
Utilities, 34

V
Vacancy rates, 35–36
Valuable consideration (specified in
    lease), 50
Vending machines, 74

W
Wholesale price index, 51

Y
Yearly operating costs, 38

Notes

Notes

Notes

Notes